THE
WELLNESS
ALMANAC

Leaping Hare Press

This edition first published in 2023 by
Leaping Hare Press
an imprint of The Quarto Group.
One Triptych Place
London, SE1 9SH
United Kingdom
T (0)20 7700 6700
www.Quarto.com

A catalogue record for this book is available from the
British Library.

ISBN 978-0-7112-9138-6
Ebook ISBN 978-0-7112-7988-9

10 9 8 7 6 5 4 3 2 1

Designer **Hanri van Wyk**
Editorial **Nayima Ali, Charlotte Frost,**
  Chloe Murphy and Elizabeth Clinton
Illustrator **Raluca Spatacean**
Senior Commissioning Editor **Monica Perdoni**

Printed in China

The information in this book is for general
informational purposes only. Tools with sharp
edges are inherently dangerous and the
instructions in this book should only be
followed by a responsible adult. Particular care
should be taken by anyone whose condition or
medication may make using such tools more
dangerous. All tools should be used and stored
in a safe and legal manner, particularly away
from children and animals and with due regard
to health and safety and good common sense. It
is essential to use non-toxic species of wood.
Special care should be taken when identifying
wood species to avoid the possibility of adverse
reactions. The publisher and the authors make
no representations or warranties of any kind,
express or implied, with respect to the accuracy,
completeness, suitability or currency of the
contents of this book, and specifically disclaim,
to the extent permitted by law, any implied
warranties of merchantability or fitness for a
particular purpose and any injury, illness,
damage, liability or loss incurred, directly or
indirectly, from the use or application of any of
the information contained in this book.

MIX
Paper | Supporting
responsible forestry
FSC® C016973

THE
WELLNESS
ALMANAC

Your Yearlong Guide to
Creating Positive Spiritual Habits

ILLUSTRATED BY
RALUCA SPATACEAN

CONTENTS

MINDFULNESS

CONNECTION

WISDOM

NATURE

INTRODUCTION

Wellness means different things to different people. It can mean feeling calm and at peace; happy and joyful; strong and resilient, or all of these things combined.

The Wellness Almanac is a big book for a reason. It brings together the very best of the lovingly created titles that have made our conscious-living list what it is, in one gloriously mindful mix.

Meditation; reflection; journalling; movement; crafting; practicing gratitude; connecting with nature; visualization and affirmation are all activities that we can incorporate into our everyday lives. The simple and soulful habits you will learn in this almanac will help strengthen your connection with creativity; nature; mindfulness; compassion; connection; and love. And who doesn't want and need more of that?

Structured around nature's seasons, this almanac is broken down into monthly sections. Each month provides mindful insights to reflect on; meditations and star-gazing practices to ground yourself; a creative step on your journalling journey towards inner understanding; a recipe or technique to realize the empowering joy of handwork; yoga and breathwork to holistically reconnect with your mind, body and spirit, gratitude notes, and visualizations and affirmations to help you tune into you, and the world around you.

Like nature's cycles, our holistic health is in constant,
meaningful change. Paying attention to our inner selves and
nurturing our feelings helps us to be more aware of the energy
we send out into this magical world.

Cultivating positive daily spiritual habits that ground us, can help free
us to notice, accept and embrace ourselves, each other and the natural
world. And this allows us to be meaningfully present in all that we do.

BE YOU; BE TRUE; BE BRAVE; BE MINDFUL; BE LIFE!

ABOUT THIS BOOK

In this lovingly crafted almanac, each spread shares a mindful insight for inner understanding, positive action, handwork, a nature-connection, and self-love.

We recommend you open this gorgeous guide as part of your morning (or evening) ritual and set a self-care intention for the day ahead, to either learn something new, remind yourself of who you are, or to simply be present.

Feel free to dip in and out to read one, or as many prompts, as you need, within the mindful space you have created. Use the ribbon with purpose to pick out the season or month ahead.

There is no right or wrong way to use this book; just use it to make time for yourself and your daily wellbeing.

Embrace the seasons, be empowered by rituals, and create positive spiritual habits all year long.

NATURE

REFLECTION

MOVEMENT

GRATITUDE

CRAFT

JOURNALLING

MEDITATION

STAR-GAZING

RECIPE

VISUALIZATION

RITUAL

JANUARY

Time to reset. Create space and time to reconnect to your inner self and to mindfully set new intentions.

CREATING OUR UNIQUE ENVIRONMENT

Houses do not need to be perfect, but we can adjust those things within our control. Mindfulness means being present in every moment. Just take a look around your space now; don't try to force any reactions, but see how you feel. What do you appreciate? Maybe the smooth, green leaves on a house plant or the comfort of a pillow get your shoulders unknotting. Maybe there's washing-up in the sink; is it bothering you enough to prioritize, or does it feel more important to finish a conversation and spend time with loved ones? Just sit with your feelings a moment; there's no right answer.

You can also get a sense of balance if you approach bigger decisions mindfully. For instance: are you contemplating changes? A new sofa or better lighting are aesthetically pleasing and can give us a mindful space, but if they put us into debt or clutter our rooms then what we have already can be enough. Again, take a moment to sit peacefully with your feelings. If you're frustrated that right now it's more sensible to keep a tatty old couch, for instance, just let that frustration flow through you. Don't fight it – it won't hurt you. Sit with it mindfully, and it will pass.

Of course, a home isn't just the objects within it; it's also what you do there. Friends in the kitchen, sharing a meal, laughter and shared memories; a shower after a long walk or a bath with a book: all these create moments to be present in. There is no right or wrong answer when considering what makes your home right for you, perhaps a well-stocked fridge, a comfy bed or a movie night every Sunday. The smell of cooking wafting through the kitchen, warmth in the winter, being safe and secure – what makes you feel content?

A home should provide you with a safe haven, a place where your emotional needs can be met and you can be yourself. Things can get overlooked when creating your space – elements that not only create a sanctuary for you but are also easy, free and within your reach. Laughter costs nothing; sleep costs nothing; relaxation is within everyone's budget. As time passes we will enter different stages of our lives, a family may grow and the way we use our space will change – just as we develop, so do our homes around us. People can get into a routine about sleeping on their side of the bed or sitting in a certain spot on the sofa but it can be good to shake things up. Rearranging and redecorating a home can bring about positive change. All that really matters is that it reflects us, our lives and our personalities; if we can do this, the rest will fall into place.

MOVEMENT

NURTURE INNER STRENGTH

DURATION: 10–15 minutes
YOGA STYLE: Classical Hatha
GOOD FOR: Strength, balance, confidence

This sequence will help you build muscular strength and connect with your potent and infinite source of inner power. The poses will help you to realize that you are powerful beyond measure and all you need to do is consciously tap into your reservoir of strength and courage. You will build your muscles, improve your balance and cultivate your connection to the inner strength that lies deep within you.

Spend 5–10 breaths in each posture (on each side when the pose is done on the left and right legs). Feel your connection to Mother Earth as you lengthen upwards towards the infinite cosmos. You are the connector between them and the power of both flows through you. Finish your practice with a 2-minute Corpse Pose to consolidate the power you have generated.

WALK CONFIDENTLY INTO YOUR DAY KNOWING THAT YOU ARE A
POWERFUL AND STRONG HUMAN BEING.

ONE ROUND WILL LOOK LIKE THIS

· Mountain Pose
· Warrior II
· Tree Pose
· Goddess Pose

1. MOUNTAIN POSE

2. WARRIOR II

3. TREE POSE

4. GODDESS POSE

FIND JOY IN GRATITUDE

Shift your perspective and see the joy in your life with this exercise.

Invest in a keepsake box and fill it with good memories, anything from photographs to mementos of days out, tickets, pictures, happy quotes, and poems. You could also write up special memories as short stories and include these in the box.

Every evening, spend some time thinking about the day and all the things you are thankful for. These could be little things, like a nice home-cooked meal or a friendly smile from a stranger, to big events. Remember to also give thanks for all the things that make you special, and for family and friends too. Write a list of these blessings on some paper and add this to your keepsake box. At the end of each week, or whenever you need a pick-me-up, dip into the box and draw something out to remind you of the joy that's present in every day.

Get into the habit of being grateful and you'll see the blessings in life more easily. You will also switch your focus from the things you feel are lacking, to all the good things you have.

I choose happiness.

Bliss is in this moment, right now.

I see the wonder in my world.

I am blessed.

RHYTHMS AND CYCLES

There is something very comforting about the regularity and predictability of the night sky. You can be sure that as people go to bed on a winter's night in the northern hemisphere, Orion and Gemini will be wheeling up into view. Or if you are in the southern hemisphere, Lyra and Sagittarius will be just rising. So many of us lead such busy, stress-filled lives, that winding down in time for bed can be quite a challenge. For those who lie awake sleepless into the small hours, these familiar patterns can be a source of reassuring, nocturnal companionship. If you find yourself lying awake with to-do lists and ideas whizzing endlessly around your mind, try opening your bedroom curtains and letting your gaze draw outwards towards the dark. Notice the rhythm of your breath, the rhythm of your heartbeat, the sway of the trees and the steady twinkling of the stars.

Hectic lives mean that our daily rhythms and routines can easily get forgotten. For many, maintaining a steady daily routine needs effort and attention. Getting up at the same time, going to bed at the same time and cooking at a reasonable hour keeps us on a steady keel.

NATURE KNOWLEDGE

Simple maintenance will give your plants the best chance of being healthy and strong. January is the ideal month to take root cuttings.

ROOT CUTTINGS

Take a healthy stout root, cut it into 5cm (2in) sections and pot it in well-drained compost with the tip of the cutting just shy of the top of the soil. Do not overwater your cuttings. Shoots should emerge in early spring.

DEADHEADING

A flower's primary goal is to set seed. If you constantly cut off the dead heads the plant goes into overdrive, sending out more flowers in an effort to reproduce, providing abundant displays all summer long.

DIVISION

To divide an overgrown plant, dig it up, remove as much of the soil from the roots as you can, and cut the plant in half with a sharp knife. Replant the parent plant in the original hole or repot the new plant in a new position. Water thoroughly before and after planting until established.

AIR CIRCULATION

Plants need good air circulation to help release waste gases and reduce the chances of disease and attack. Space plants according to size, which aids circulation and prevents competing for nutrients and soil water.

PRUNING

Cutting back dead, damaged or diseased parts of the plant encourages growth and helps maintain vigour. Do this in spring or autumn, according to the type of plant, and either compost the prunings or, if diseased, destroy them on a fire (use the ashes to condition the soil with potassium).

THE WRITING ADVENTURE

Our pens are like magic wands – with a swirl and a dash and a few dots we create meaning through words. How wonderful! But this process is often easier said than done. As writers, we need to develop an awareness that is unusually acute: the touch of raindrops on our face, the scent of grass, the simple action of taking a breath. Such attentiveness does not exclude those who seek the lucidity of an articulate, thinking mind. On the contrary, it is through such conscious awareness that the writer comes to a clear understanding of their own abilities, needs and preferences.

Stop for a minute and recognize how your feet connect with the ground at this moment. If you are sitting, notice the weight of your own body supported by the chair. Be aware of the air entering and leaving your body as you breathe. Touch your face, or your hair. Notice the way this feels without judging or analyzing.

Similarly, when we write, we can try truly to appreciate the complete wonder of how our hand transfers thoughts into tangible, observable ideas – the reality of words on the page. So, the writer is a kind of magician, and the pen is a wand of power.

TAKE UP YOUR PEN

Become aware of its weight and capacity to transform. Think of the potential stories, poems and other writings that will emerge from it. This is the beginning of the writing adventure.

CLOUDY MIND, CLEAR MIND

When we meditate, our concentration can suffer from bad 'seeing'.
You might say our focus 'twinkles' as we are bombarded by endless
thoughts, impressions, perceptions, memories and ideas. How do we
deal with these distractions? The first thing is to realize that everyone
gets them. It is not just you. When we stop and take a moment to
look inside our minds, it can feel like complete chaos. That's fine.
Mindfulness is not about getting rid of these thoughts; instead, what it
teaches us is how to change our attitude or relationship to them.

If we envisage a thought like a cloud in the sky, then we know there
are times when there are lots of clouds and times when there are few.
Sometimes it is totally overcast – our mind is so busy that thoughts
are crowding in one after another with no space in between. Maybe
it is like that for you your whole working day. Sometimes there are
just a few white fluffy clouds scudding overhead. Sometimes the sky
clears completely. But having a clear mind is as rare as a blue sky in a
rainforest; it is lovely when it happens, but chasing it gets us nowhere.
Our job is to accept and allow things just as they are. Let the mind be
as cloudy or clear as it is right now, and bring an attitude of kindness
and patience to your experience. Even on the cloudiest of nights, the
stars are still shining. Even when our mind is racing, we can allow that
busyness and acknowledge that it is fine.

People liken mindfulness to a trip to the gym for your mind. Every time
we get involuntarily whisked away from our focus and start following
a train of thought, we gently guide our awareness back to the here and
now. There is no need to try and work out why you were distracted or to
chastise yourself. Just come back to now.

RUNNING STITCH

Running stitch is the simplest of stitches and the basis of all hand sewing.

TOOLS AND MATERIALS

- Needle threaded with 1 x 40cm (15¾in) length of cotton thread
- Small piece of fabric

METHOD

1. Knot the end of your thread and bring the needle through from the back of the fabric to the front so the knot stays in the back.

2. Take the needle forwards one stitch length, push the tip through to the back, scoop up one stitch length of fabric and push the needle back through to the front. Grasp the pointed end of the needle and pull the needle all the way through until the thread is taut.

3. Move forwards one stitch length and repeat this process.

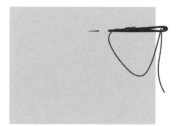

4. Once you gain confidence, you can load multiple stitches onto your needle in one go, moving from front to back, to front to back.

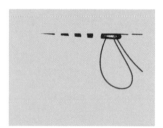

5. When you have finished stitching, bring your needle through to the back, take a small stitch on the spot, pulling it through only enough to leave a small loop. Pass the needle though the loop and pull the thread tight. Repeat and cut the thread, leaving a 1.3cm (½in) tail.

LISTEN TO THE FALLING RAIN

Without water in some form, we cannot garden. Wells and moisture stored in the soil through permaculture techniques are very useful, but what a garden needs, at least to some degree, is rain. Rain brings not only non-chlorinated water, but each drop also contains a particle of soil. Rain clouds and storms carry soil around the Earth, sharing minerals with gardens downstream. Rain connects us to everyone else on Earth.

Rain brings life. Too much rain, though, is problematic. So rain teaches us about the nourishing gifts of nature but also about balance and gratitude. We hope for just the right amount of rain, and when it comes we are filled with a sense of things being right in the world. Before plumbing, rain and various aqueduct systems were all we had to water our fields. Drought meant death, and even the end of whole civilizations. In parts of Africa and Asia, this is still true. It is no wonder that across many cultures we find rain gods or guardians, like Dudumitsa from Bulgaria, the Yoruban Oya and Aztec Tlaloc.

Rain, both literal and metaphorical, is mentioned throughout the Bible. Rain is life. We are learning, too, that even in industrialized, developed nations, we cannot just do whatever we like with rain and the rest of the planet's water. Draining aquifers faster than they can replenish, we are upsetting the balance of the planet's life-giving water. Perhaps we need to return to water management practices based on mindful gratitude.

Water is life.
I am life.
All is one.

TAKE A NIGHT WALK

In the midst of the city, we experience a night that could not be further from the one our ancestors enjoyed, with nothing more than a small fire and the stars for illumination once the sun set. These 24/7 lifestyles we've developed have, arguably, helped us to achieve more in a day, but they certainly come at a price. Experiencing the dark is good for us; it is natural to our biology, crucial for restorative sleep and keeps our immune system functioning. Living in a place that barely sleeps can, therefore, be a draining aspect of urban living.

Ensuring that we have as much time as possible in the quiet and dark is a mindful exercise we can practise at home, by making these environments less stimulating than the streets outside. Keeping evenings as calm and low-lit as possible is within our control, and we can switch off phones, TVs, computers and lamps, all of which can be disruptive to the body's biology when we sleep. We can then better appreciate the city at night when we are out there, experience it in a positive way as opposed to a mental drain. Our mind is less charged, more open to seeing the city at night as beautiful in its own way. Open to observe more, we see the changing colours of the darkening sky and take in the aromas of exotic foods drifting out from restaurant kitchens.

MERE FLICKERS

Taking a night walk with the distinct purpose of aimlessness reveals features of the city's personality special to that time of day. As we walk, we can glimpse the moon above us. Turning our eyes upwards to see this postmark of another dimension, one beyond the city limits, is a reminder of our place in the solar system. Far from making us feel insignificant as we consider how brief our lives are compared with the eternal space the moon inhabits, glancing at the moon allows us to reflect on the precious nature of the now. Reminding ourselves, every once in a while, that we are mere flickers in the life of a planet over four billion years old can be an uplifting, life-affirming meditation – one that motivates us to feel thankful that we were ever present to experience it at all.

RAW CHOCOLATE BROWNIES

This is the perfect moist, indulgent brownie recipe, an ideal treat for a cosy winter night. With a base made from walnuts and almonds, it's a delicious alternative to the classic cake.

MAKES 20

INGREDIENTS

- 150g (5¹/₂oz) raw whole almonds
- 100g (3¹/₂oz) raw coconut oil, melted (see page 340)
- 50g (1³/₄oz) raw cacao powder
- 400g (14oz) fresh dates, stoned and chopped widthways into 3 pieces
- 125g (4¹/₂oz) raw walnut halves
- 3 heaped tsp xylitol crystals, plus extra for sprinkling
- pinch of pink crystal salt
- 20g (³/₄oz) yacon syrup
- 50ml (2fl oz) fresh filtered water

EQUIPMENT

- food processor or power blender
- wooden spoon (optional)
- large mixing bowl
- 20 x 22cm (8 x 8¹/₂in) silicone cake mould
- chopping board
- knife

METHOD

1. Process the almonds in your food processor or powder blender until roughly ground.

2. Add the coconut oil, cacao powder, dates, 75g (2³/₄oz) of the walnuts, the xylitol crystals and salt to the almonds in the food processor. Process until all ingredients are completely broken down, stopping the food processor to stir the ingredients with the spoon if necessary, just to help it along. You should have a thick, brown mixture when it's done.

3. Spoon the mixture into a large mixing bowl and stir in the remaining walnuts, the yacon syrup and water until it turns sticky.

4. Spoon into the cake mould, making sure that the mixture reaches each side of the mould, including the corners. Use the back of the spoon to smooth the top of the mixture evenly.

5. Place in the freezer for 30 minutes or until firm but not frozen.

6. Take the cake out of the freezer and peel the sides of the mould away from the cake to loosen it slightly. While the cake is still quite firm from being in the freezer, lift it straight out onto a chopping board and sprinkle lightly with xylitol crystals to decorate. Slice into roughly 4-cm (1¹/₂-in) squares and either serve immediately or keep them refrigerated, covered, for up to 3 days.

TIP

The brownies can be served with ice cream as a dessert or cut into slightly smaller pieces and served as a sweet canapé.

THE CREATIVE PATH

We live in a time where we need to connect with our creative selves more than ever. The unending stimulation of the modern world can be overwhelming, but it also offers opportunities for creative inspiration – if only we can draw breath long enough to soak it up and express what we make of it all. As a society, we seem to be tuning in to the rich benefits that art has to offer us as human beings. A surge of creativity is being embraced the world over, with more people taking up all sorts of art practices for pleasure and wellbeing. In this inherent form of self-expression is a vast array of rewards, and the benefits are richly enhanced when we incorporate mindfulness with our artistic practice.

Art provides for a mindful practitioner a stimulating focus with which to hone and cultivate inner stillness. Delicately and dexterously manipulating nothing into something requires us to reach somewhere beyond the external world into the inner realm where our imagination thrives. By learning to delve deeper into this space we enrich both our meditation and our art. The wealth and beauty of making can go unnoticed, be forgotten or diluted if you aren't present to experience it in the moment. When we create in a mindful way, we can witness the transformation that our creativity brings. Our minds can open to a more intuitive and playful way of making, leading us to a greater sense of joy. We can connect intimately and compassionately with ourselves and others.

By quietening the babble of our conscious mind and letting go of control we can allow our whispered inspirations to be heard and respond to them without fear. Through mindfulness we can rise above the damning inner critic with confidence in our artistic ability.

For many of us, having time to make art can be something of a luxury. When we find these moments, we owe it to ourselves to leave behind day-to-day concerns and to be fully present. When we connect deeply with our craft through mindful awareness, we open ourselves up to the magic of making and the beauty that can be found in the here and now.

FEBRUARY

Time to explore. Seek out fresh air, new pathways and naturescapes to bring together mind, body and soul in one joyful experience.

JUST WALK

One of the kindest things we can do for ourselves is to go for a good walk. It is one of the most natural activities in the world, exercising the body and stimulating the heart, while at the same time freeing the mind to become more open and alert. Like an over-tight muscle, the mind needs to be loosened before it can let go, so we are then able to enjoy the present moment and face reality. We return from a successful walk refreshed and clear-headed.

We may use walking as a way to increase our levels of awareness and to improve our conscious living – to make the walk more enjoyable as we come to understand our place in the world of nature. The questions that lurk at the back of the mind can be faced: Who am I? Where have I come from? Where am I going? The walking may involve no more than a daily gentle stroll, or it may extend to that well-planned great hike that takes us beyond the horizon, following the course of a great river, or over mountain ranges and through remote forests.

Mindfulness is a way to keep in touch with reality, important for each of us individually, but also as members of a powerful and potentially destructive species. As an exercise, it has its roots both in human nature and in Buddhism. It is not always easy to be a human being; increasingly, we are in danger of living lives of fevered anxiety, concerned about the past and worried about the future, forgetting the life that is to be found here and now. We feel that in growing older we have lost something, that innocent ability in childhood to take unquestioning delight in simple things – a ladybird, a toy or a gift.

THE IMPORTANCE OF BREATHWORK

DURATION: 5–7 minutes
YOGA STYLE: All styles
GOOD FOR: Focus

Yoga is the union of body and mind and it is through the breath that we unite them. The focussed and conscious use of breath is what defines yoga and differentiates it from other forms of physical stretching, such as post-workout cool-down stretches.

Before you begin the pranayama practice opposite, sit in a comfortable position, close your eyes and focus for 1–2 minutes on your breath. Observe its natural rhythm, flow and where you can feel it in your body.

1. Place one hand on your belly and one on your chest.

2. Inhale into your belly and feel this area rise.

3. Carry on filling your lungs and feel your chest rise.

4. To exhale, release the air from your chest and then your belly.

5. Squeeze out all the air using your abdominal muscles.

Repeat for 3–10 rounds.

At no point should you hold your breath. A general rule for breathing in yoga is to inhale when you open or expand the body and exhale when you fold or contract.

GRATITUDE FOR THE WAY THINGS ARE

The practice of gratitude is an important aspect of mindfulness. Make a mental note of three things in your life you are grateful for. You can include things as simple as having heating or clean water, or as profound as having a loving partner, caring friends or constantly being under Earth's protective wing. If you do this exercise every day you will notice that some of the things you are grateful for will recur, while others may come and go, but gradually your perspective on the world will change. Gratitude helps us to feel more positive and replaces our wants, desires and drives with a sense of contentment with how things are in our lives right now.

*I vow to accept my
life for what it is
and be grateful
for what I have.*

WHY SWAP SEEDS?

Seed swapping is a means of exchanging surplus seeds as a goodwill gesture, and usually takes place at organized gatherings for novice and seasoned gardeners. Participants trade their seeds and knowledge in a local community hall or someone's house, or even via a 'round robin'.

With the increase in the cost of living, seed swapping is a great way of becoming more self-sufficient in the ornamental garden as well as the fruit and vegetable garden. Saving and swapping seeds has a wealth of benefits, from financial savings through to maintaining food security and protecting biodiversity, rare species and seed genetics. It also helps to disseminate the practices and ideas of other cultures, which may be linked to particular plant species. Seeds have the ability to travel great distances, and those with the greatest cultural significance tend to get transported by people as they move around the globe.

Swapping seeds expands plant variety in a 'swapper's' garden. At seed swaps, a wealth of local knowledge and wisdom can be exchanged, about what works – or doesn't work – in your microclimate, and you are likely to discover new and exciting plants. Keeping things 'local' helps the community become independent from seed manufacturers who tend to have control over the availability and variety of seeds. Although seed saving has a long history, global events like Seedy Saturday and Seedy Sunday only began in 1990.

Seasoned seed-swap gardeners incorporate collecting seeds into their gardening routine specifically for seed-swapping events, and the ever-increasing popularity of these occasions has gained the interest of keen novices too.

START A ROUND ROBIN SEED SWAP

If you can't meet in person, why not start a seed-swapping chain. Keep it local; you are more likely to find plants that are happy growing in the conditions provided by your local climate.

1. Collect names and addresses of the willing participants and provide the final list of names to everyone involved.

2. As the organizer, send a package filled with your surplus seeds to the next person on the list.

3. The next person will then take one packet of seeds from the package and replace them with some more seeds.

4. The package is sent to the next person on the list, who removes and replaces as above.

5. The chain carries on until the last person on the list posts the package (which should now contain a completely different combination of seeds) back to the original organizer.

NATURE

SEEDSAVING:
THE ENVIRONMENTAL BENEFITS

WILDLIFE

Saving seeds saves species. Plant diversity supports wildlife diversity, and together they create a healthy ecosystem that is fundamental to the existence of all living things. The US Fish and Wildlife Service estimates that losing one plant species can trigger the loss of up to 30 other insect, plant and animal species.

FOOD DIVERSITY

Conserving seeds is conserving food diversity and a diverse range of crops. It took 10,000 years to develop the agricultural diversity we enjoy today, and this is being threatened by global food industries whose single aim is profit. As a result, we have hyper-productive, hyper-durable plant varieties in place of organically grown, open-pollinated plants.

Food diversity is plummeting into a world of mono-cropping. The seed-saving community is seed activism at its best, a worldwide group effort to preserve plant diversity.

COMMUNITY

Swapping your saved seeds strengthens community links. It's a great way of making new friends and there will probably be lots of interesting conversations you can earwig or join in with. At seed swaps there are often talks and workshops on related subjects, such as beekeeping, wildflowers, rare plants, biodiversity and even how to cook with your home produce.

FOOD SECURITY

Seed savers sow the seeds of food security by growing and eating their own produce. This means that their produce doesn't have far to travel from plot to plate, and gardeners have control over which foods they grow, to suit their culture and diet. Being able to save seeds from your own garden secures a food supply for you, for future generations of your family and for the community with which you seed swap.

SEEDS: PROMISES AND HOPES

A seed is the epitome of hope. Inside a seed rests 'life concentrate'. Everything a plant needs to reach first down into the darkness and then upwards towards the light is held safe in the hard containment of the seed coat. Inside the suitcase of the seed coat waits a tiny future root, a tiny future shoot and all the food the seedling will need to get started. Also inside the little package of life are invisible instructions telling the seed just what it's here to do.

As gardeners, we use seeds as prayers, little promises of what is to come. We humans eat seeds daily: rice, wheat, sunflower, pea, bean, peanut, sesame . . . Some seeds are harder to digest than others, as a seed wants to be not consumed but continued, carried on. Some of us can't digest certain seeds at all; some bodies read gluten as a toxin, so reject wheat, rye or barley seeds in any form. Perhaps the surge of allergies to various seeds is the planet's way of urging us to respect seeds: stop taking them for granted; stop dousing them with poisons; stop modifying them – respect them.

WHAT SEEDS ARE NEAR YOU AT THIS MOMENT?

Seeds are all around us. They are all around us because seeds are life; seeds are nourishment; seeds are promises and hopes for the future. Look around you, what seeds are nearby at this moment?

NOT JUST A METAPHOR

For a gardener who starts at least some plants from seeds, a pile of seeds invokes a giddy excitement. Seeds mean spring and the garden. To the farmer in Malawi or rural India, seeds mean they and their children will live another year. For them, the seed is not just a metaphor. And really, the same is true for us all. In developed nations, we can forget that our lives depend on seeds. This is why seed banks around the world store a variety of rare and common seeds, keeping them safe for the benefit of humanity as well as the plants.

In 2015, Syrian agricultural researchers made the first withdrawal of seeds from the Svalbard Global Seed Vault – sometimes referred to as 'the doomsday vault' – since its creation in 2008. The seeds were planted in Morocco and Lebanon, after the drought-resistant varieties of wheat were destroyed by the conflict in Syria. We are all united by our reliance on plants and their seeds. By growing, protecting and saving seeds yourself, you are a part of this web that reaches across all cultural barriers. The seeds that keep us alive depend on us to do the same for them.

EXPLORING YOUR INNER VOICE

Through genetics and experience, we become who we are to the world. But who are we to ourselves? Very often, we don't really say the things we want to say. Even if we are known as great talkers, there can be a silence inside, blocking our real voice. People think they know us but we may just be trying to please them, or to impress them, or to display a false cover in order to protect our true selves.

So that we can write with honesty, clarity and joy, we need to get in touch with that voice inside. Sometimes it's buried so deep that we have to dig a little (but gently!) in order to find it. This is an exercise in exploration, and it can be very rewarding.

The exercise on the page opposite relates to your inner feelings, memories and emotions. Because of this, it is best to keep your writing to yourself. This is because privacy can assist us in working out our true feelings. If others are involved, we will probably take their needs and opinions into account. And this exploration is just for you.

1. Sit as comfortably as possible with this book, a piece of paper and a pen or pencil in front of you. Put your feet flat on the floor if possible. Notice how it feels to have the soles of your feet connecting with the ground.

2. Turn your attention to your breathing. Notice the air entering and leaving your body; it's usually cooler as it enters your nose or mouth, and warmer as it leaves.

3. If thoughts try to disturb you, just acknowledge them but bring your attention back to your breath.

4. After a few minutes, place your hand on the open page of this book. Connect with how that feels, without analyzing or judging.

5. Pick up your pen or pencil. Feel the weight of it in your hand.

6. Now, answer the questions below. Take a calm breath in and out before and after reading each question, so that your answer comes from a place of clarity.

Which activities give you most pleasure?

Which place do you like best?

What is your favourite memory?

Which subject did you enjoy most at school?

CRAFT

MAKE YOUR OWN
AIR-DRYING CLAY

To enhance your mindful crafting experiences, why not have a go at making your own air-drying clay from scratch? This simple clay dries to a lovely opaque white, but be careful as it is quite fragile.

MAKES APPROX. 500G (1LB 1¹/₂OZ)

TOOLS AND MATERIALS

- 240ml (8¹/₂fl oz) water
- 128g (4¹/₂oz) cornflour (cornstarch)
- 256g (9oz) bicarbonate of soda (baking soda)
- non-stick saucepan
- silicone cake mould
- clingfilm (plastic wrap)

TIP

*Wrap any unused
pieces of air-drying clay
in clingfilm (plastic wrap).
This will stop the clay from
drying out and allow it to
be used again.*

METHOD

1. Stir all the ingredients together in a non-stick saucepan.

2. Put the saucepan over a low heat, and cook for a few minutes, stirring continuously. When the mixture changes from a soft paste to a thicker consistency, similar to porridge, remove the saucepan from the heat.

3. Transfer the dough into the silicone cake mould and keep it covered until the dough has cooled down. Keep the clay well wrapped when not using. You can store the clay in the fridge for 1–2 weeks.

REFLECTION

WAITING FOR SPRING

One of the most moving of natural phenomena in the avian world is the regular spring migration in the northern hemisphere, when immense flocks of birds wing their way north to their breeding grounds. Waves of birds roll up through the Americas; they flood across Asia, through Vietnam and Korea; they flow from Africa to Europe. Knowledge of this vast pageant stirs the human spirit year by year, inducing a sense of humility that we are part of a greater picture, observers of a magical process of renewal.

We cannot isolate the changing behaviour of birds in the spring from everything else that happens in that season. The sun rises higher in the sky, warming the ground. We breathe the fresh milder air, see leaves beginning to unfold and feel the rising sap of life. Spring is in fact more than simply the regeneration of nature, it is a symbol of rebirth and personal renewal.

SPRING ARRIVALS

The nineteenth-century American poet, philosopher and naturalist Henry D. Thoreau, living in the woods by Walden Pond seeking, as he puts it, 'the tonic of wildness', listens out for the signs of spring with eager anticipation: the cracking of the ice on the pond, the sound of geese migrating north, and the singing from the fields of the bluebird, song sparrow and redwing. Thoreau's response to the birds of spring is matched by that of the wilderness sage John Muir, the Scotsman who toiled so hard to save America's wild places, founding father of its national parks. The bluebird is for him, too, the long-awaited spring arrival, heralding with its 'rich crispy warbling' a fresh year of growth and vitality.

Each of us, depending where we live, has different expectations of what birds to listen and look for. In Europe, it may be the sound of the skylark ascending above his nesting site, his winter song (a short fruity warble) transformed into a continuous flood of fluting melody from high in the sky. The lovely trickling notes of a willow warbler can bring us to a temporary standstill, enthralled. We will listen for the convivial twitter of swallows as they explore beams and roof spaces for their nests. And we will hear the cuckoo, announcing his presence with his two-tone call from some distant tree. We may forget for the moment that his long journey from Africa began in what for us was the cold and dark of midwinter. He, with all the other migratory visitors, anticipated spring, as we do, weeks before it burst in bank and hedgerow.

MEDITATIONS ON A STAR

Here is something you can try the next time you are looking up at the night sky.

Pick a star and focus all your attention on it. You might want to look slightly to the side of the star, as the very centre of your retina is less sensitive in low light. Let the experience of looking at the star be so intent that there is no room for anything else. Let 'you' looking at the 'star' become 'you–star'. This is equivalent to a narrowing, focusing type of meditation of the kind that allows the mind to quieten down into a state of peace and tranquillity.

Now try softening and broadening your gaze, and become aware of your peripheral vision. Let as many other stars, clouds, trees and buildings come into your awareness as you can. This is akin to a broad, open kind of meditation that helps us to develop kindness and patience through our experience.

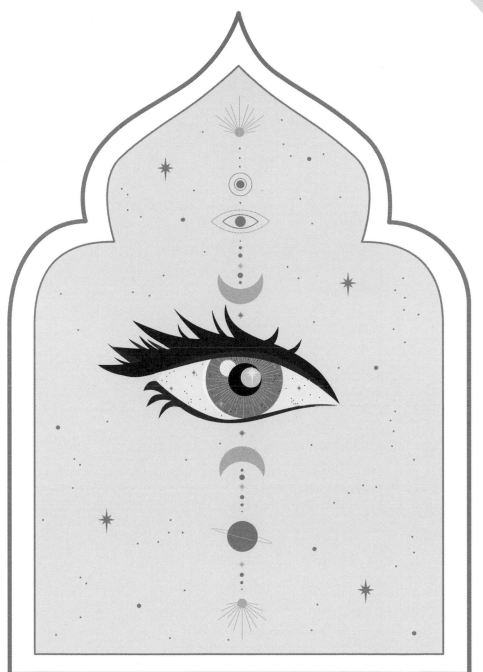

LOVE MACARONS

These delicious heart-shaped delights create chunky, raw chocolate-flavoured cakes, perfect for an afternoon tea or celebration.

MAKES 8

INGREDIENTS

- 150g (5^1/$_2$oz) raw pecan nuts
- 50g (1^3/$_4$oz) raw almonds
- pinch of pink crystal salt
- 150g (5^1/$_2$oz) fresh dates, stoned and halved widthways
- 2 tbsp raw cacao powder
- ^{1}/$_4$ tsp ground cinnamon
- 50ml (2fl oz) fresh filtered water

FOR THE FILLING

- 40g (1^1/$_2$oz) raw cacao butter
- 1 tbsp raw coconut oil
- 70g (2^1/$_2$oz) stoned, peeled avocado
- 2 tbsp xylitol crystals
- 5 drops vanilla extract
- 2 heaped tbsp raw cacao powder
- 1 heaped tbsp lucuma powder

EQUIPMENT

- food processor
- metal spoon
- two 8-hole heart-shaped silicone cake moulds
- dehydrator with mesh screen
- bain-marie
- power blender
- BPA-free plastic container

METHOD

1. Process the pecan nuts and almonds with the salt in your food processor until roughly ground.

2. Add all the other ingredients for the macarons, except the water, to the ground nuts in the food processor and begin to process. While the machine is running, slowly add the water through the chute. Process until a sticky mixture forms.

3. Spoon the mixture into each hole of the heart-shaped cake moulds until no more than 1cm (¹/₂in) in depth. Press down with the back of the spoon or your fingers to flatten to the edges.

4. Place the moulds on a mesh screen in your dehydrator and dehydrate at 40.5°C (105°F) for 1 hour. After this time the heart shapes should be a little more solid so that you can carefully pop them out of the moulds, while maintaining their beautiful shape, directly onto the screen. Dehydrate for a further 3 hours.

5. When the hearts are almost ready to retrieve from your dehydrator, melt the cacao butter gently, together with the coconut oil if it has hardened and turned white, in a bain-marie until runny.

6. Add the melted cacao butter and coconut oil, along with all the remaining filling ingredients to your power blender and blend on high power, using the plunger, until you have a smooth, creamy paste.

7. Remove the macarons from the dehydrator and top 8 of the hearts with about 4 teaspoons of the filling. Sandwich the remaining 8 hearts on top and press down gently until the filling starts to seep out of the sides. Enjoy straight away while still warm. The macarons can be stored in the airtight container in the refrigerator for up to 1 week, although the filling will harden once they have been refrigerated.

BOOST YOUR MINDSET

Invest in a quartz crystal to help you maintain clarity and focus in life.

Spend five minutes every day holding it in both of your hands. As you breathe in, imagine drawing the sparkling energy of the crystal inside you. To boost the positive effect, picture yourself cocooned in a crystal chamber. As you breathe out, pour any fear or confusion into the crystal.

At least once a week, take the crystal outside and bury it in the soil so that any negative energy can be absorbed by the earth and transformed into light. If you don't have access to a garden, then simply bury the crystal in a plant pot overnight.

Once cleansed, you can pop the crystal beneath your pillow at night and ask for guidance in your dreams.

Quartz crystal amplifies and also transmits energy, making it the perfect stone to work with when you want to release negative energy and clear the mind. Breathing with the crystal helps to calm and focus the mind.

Everything is crystal clear.

I see, I think, I am.

Clarity is mine from this moment in time.

LIVING IN
THE HERE AND NOW

A good time to practise mindfulness is when our minds are reeling. At this point, our normally overactive thinking mind is preoccupied with cooling its circuits, giving our more direct, experiencing mind a chance to feel and sense.

When we are doing walking meditation, we can feel our feet lift up, swing through and come softly to the ground. Knowing about gravity and space-time doesn't help us experience that reality; it hinders it. To directly touch our reality we have to put aside our ideas about it and realize that these words are just human-made labels to help us understand and relate to our experience. What is time? Hasn't the past already gone and the future not happened yet? There is only now and here. When we remember the past, we do it in the present. Equally when we plan the future we do it in the present. Those light rays that have been travelling through the Universe for 13 billion years know nothing of their history. They arrive now and deliver their information now. All of history, past and future, exists only now.

This is why how we live right now is so important. It is all we have. Apple co-founder Steve Jobs would apparently ask himself every day, 'If this were my last day, would I do what I'm about to do today?' and if the answer was 'no' for too many days in a row then he would reassess his plans. So, how are you going to live today?

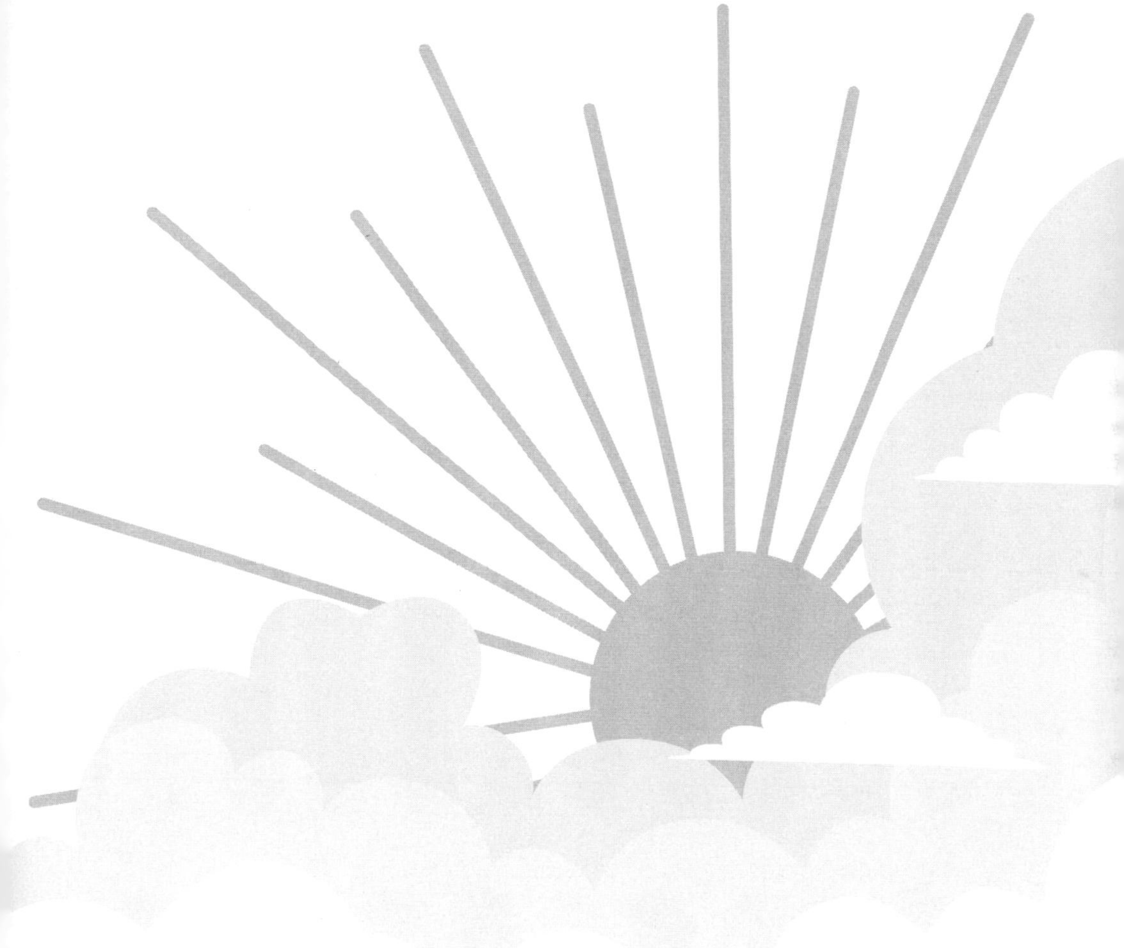

SPRING

MARCH

APRIL

MAY

SPRING PLAYLIST

· *Here Comes the Sun* – The Beatles

· *Daydream In Blue* – I Monster

· *Arrival of the Birds* – The Cinematic Orchestra

· *Spring* – Bill Callahan

· *Spring 1* – Max Richter

· *Seasons of Your Day* – Mazzy Star

· *The First Days of Spring* – Noah And The Whale

*I sow seeds of intention
for new beginnings.*

*I honour myself, the seasons
and the cycles of life.*

*Everything is in flux. The only
constant in life is change.*

MARCH

Time to talk. Baking cake, brewing tea and conversations with friends can be the best meditations.

REFLECTION

BRIGHTENING YOUR DAY

Opening your home to more natural sunlight provides many benefits to your health and to the planet; it can make you warmer, more comfortable and happier. But bringing light inside our minds is just as important as bringing light into our homes. There's a reason why we talk about 'brightening your day'.

By shining a light on our internal emotional landscape, we can pick up where we are feeling stressed and where we need space. Part of reaching a better balance is to recognize where our limits are. This is a conscious choice based on an understanding of what is healthy for us right now – not going into our emotions repeatedly and ruminating but simply recognising them as they arise. This helps us to develop some emotional agility and bring some illumination into our daily lives. We can use various methods to create more peaceful and positive experiences.

When you find yourself going through the autopilot mechanics of your daily routine, take five minutes to think about initiating positive emotions. This will more than likely help to add some sparkle to the day ahead, whatever it may bring. Combine this with opening the blinds and the curtains, and we will have a significant chance of more calm in the home.

*Morning sky, morning world,
today will be a bright new day.*

A YOGA SEQUENCE TO GREET THE DAY

DURATION: 10–12 minutes
YOGA STYLE: Vinyasa yoga
GOOD FOR: Waking up the body

Rise and shine like the sun as you move through this morning Vinyasa routine, which will wake you up and boost your energy and focus for the day.

Flow smoothly from one pose to the next, spending 2–3 breaths in each pose (or 4–6 if you are new to yoga). Remember that alignment is more important than speed. Perform 2 more rounds then set your intention for the day.

ONE ROUND WILL LOOK LIKE THIS

- Mountain Pose
- Upward Salute
- Standing Forward Fold
- Downward Facing Dog

1. MOUNTAIN POSE

2. UPWARD SALUTE

3. STANDING

FORWARD FOLD

4. DOWNWARD FACING DOG

GRATITUDE FOR THE GARDEN

A good way to stop anxiety in its tracks is to feel gratitude. Feeling a sense of thankfulness and even wonder for our lives is a form of mindfulness, which is why this works to halt anxiety. Even severe anxiety, as in a panic attack, lessens its grip a little when we sit mindfully with what is happening right now. I am alive. I am feeling sensations that I don't like, but I am feeling.

Remember this when you're next feeling cranky about your garden. Perhaps something has died, or it's not yet time to plant, or you only have one measly grape on the vine. While you can allow yourself to feel frustration and disappointment, you can also shift your perspective just a little to include gratitude. That one grape is really very pretty, and this grape vine is still alive. You have soil in which to plant a grape vine. You have a garden in which to cultivate that soil. Then your single grape becomes a celebration, instead of a whine fest.

Gardening lends
itself to gratitude. Each
day there is something new
emerging in the world: a new
leaf, a cluster of ladybird eggs or
the first violets of spring. What
are you grateful for?

SLOW FOOD
IN A FAST WORLD

Cooking is surely one of the most pleasurable activities we engage in on a daily basis. It is an activity that satisfies our need to 'do' at a practical level and offers a sensory and aesthetic challenge. It has the potential to be social: the preparation can be teamwork, the results shared. Making things to eat is one of those daily tasks that is perfect for developing a more 'mindful' approach to life. Cooking is easily within our grasp and ready to benefit from a dose of slowing down and a gentle regime of awareness-building. Whatever we cook, it will turn out better if it is prepared in the absence of stress and with plenty of time.

THE JOY OF COOKING

Let's welcome in the deep meditative pleasure of cooking and being joyfully alive in the heart of our homes. Feeling the empowerment that comes as we create, improvise, share and engage in the sanity of small tasks that bring balance to our day.

Back in 1931 when Irma Rombauer published the very first edition of America's classic guide *The Joy of Cooking*, there were very few gadgets to do the job for us. Preparing food was a quiet activity, and the ingredients, although limited, were for the main part wholesome and unsprayed. In fact, some of the processes involved were very meditative practices for a mindful cook of today: rubbing cooked vegetables or fruit through a sieve to create a purée rather than using a food processor, or making pastry and bread from scratch rather than buying them readymade. The title is itself revealing. For a tenacious widow who was recovering from her husband's recent death, the decision to embark on the task of writing a cookbook that would become best friend to many American housewives shows that cooking itself is a great domain in which to find renewal.

THE ART OF NURTURE

Cooking offers us the opportunity to practise the nourishment of ourselves and others. Let's make it easy – as easy as possible – for us to show ourselves for who we are. In the security of our own homes, let's do what we can to support the flowering of the person we feel ourselves to truly be, rather than the person we feel others think we ought to be. Let's forget about the way we present ourselves and get down to nurturing our soul.

CULTIVATING GOOD PRACTICE

When it comes to serving up the food that nourishes, a familiar environment imbued with the warmth of loved ones may be the best ambience. Equally, though, imagine yourself arriving at the end of a long and arduous pilgrimage to be welcomed by complete strangers with bowls of warm soup. You might never have been in such a home as theirs before, you might never have smelt such a soup, yet their beaming, friendly eyes and keenness to help might lead you to feel the replenishing nurture of the warm food reviving you. Put aside any thoughts of whether this food was made with ingredients you approve of and think only of your body's need for nourishment and the health and goodwill of those looking after you. So why not try cooking a recipe that engages you in this transformative journey?

AURIGA

LATIN FOR : *charioteer*

Auriga is part of the Perseus group of constellations that are connected to the Perseus myth. It is known as 'the Charioteer' and was so named because its brightest stars (including Capella and Menkalinan) formed a shape that reminded the Romans of the pointed helmet of a charioteer.

Auriga is the site of the Galactic Anticenter, the point in the sky directly opposite the Galactic Center as viewed from Earth. The Galactic Centre is the centre of our Milky Way galaxy (located in the constellation Sagittarius). Because it is located on the band of the Milky Way, Auriga has many bright open clusters within its borders that are easy targets for amateur telescopes. It also hosts Capella (α Aurigae), the sixth-brightest star in the night sky.

BEST TIME TO OBSERVE

Auriga calls to mind the shepherds who stay with their flocks on the hillside for months at a time, living in tune with nature and the seasons, and likely very knowledgeable about the night sky. The life of a shepherd must be tough and often lonely, but their job is simple – take care of the flock. Today, many of us crave a life more like this: simpler, in contact with nature, and time to just sit and be. When life gets busy it's often these simple things that we cut out first. But when we stop doing things that nourish us, we become depleted and stressed. Auriga can remind us to be more shepherd-like – simplify things, take time and notice the rhythms of life.

TIME WITH THE SENSES

1. Stop and take a couple of quiet breaths. Close your eyes for a moment and then open them again. What do you see? What is ahead of you, and what is on the periphery of your vision?

2. Concentrate on your hearing. Even in a quiet room there may be something in the distance: a clock chiming, the sound of your own heart beating.

3. What are you touching? Think about what you can feel even without actively touching – a breeze, the chair you are sitting on, some physical sensation.

4. Can you taste anything? Tea, perhaps? The lingering flavour of your last meal?

5. Give attention to your sense of smell. This is often the neglected or unnoticed sense. Are there any obvious scents around you? If not, cup your hands over your nose and mouth and describe what you can smell.

WRITE DOWN

What I love to see

What I love to hear

What I love to touch

What I love to taste

What I love to smell

REFLECTION

ROOTS

Gardeners are always putting down roots. The plants we partner with stretch their own roots deep into the soil in search of nourishment and water. In tending the plants, we also put down roots energetically wherever we garden. People who relocate to new houses often feel more grounded to a place by planting even a few herbs in a pot on the patio or windowsill. Farmers, of course, root their families so deeply to place that it becomes a part of who they are.

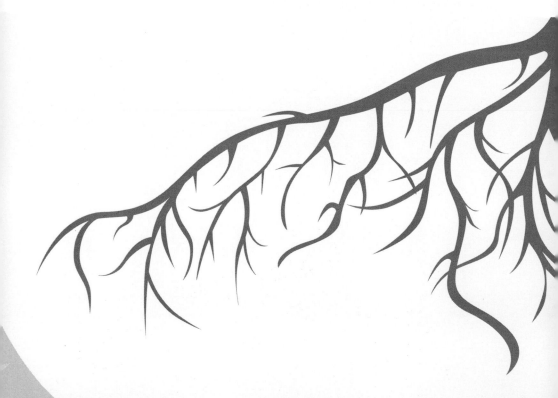

The longer the lifespan of the plant, the greater the sense of connection and commitment to the land. By planting asparagus, fruit trees or roses, for example, you sign up for a long-term relationship with the land. As you tend the soil, the land supports you. If your garden contains edibles, you literally become a part of the land as you consume the gifts of the earth. This connection through gardens is true of communities as well as individuals. When neighbours create a community garden, they create common ground. We all ground through putting down roots.

ROOT MEDITATION

Sit in a place where you will not be disturbed. Outside is best, but not necessary. Sitting with your back against a tree or near a favourite plant would be a perfect place to practise this meditation on your own roots, but sitting on the floor indoors or even on a chair is fine. Close your eyes and feel your sitting bones press into the ground. Notice how the ground presses back against you. Now reach your awareness past this connection, sensing into the space below you. Reach your awareness down until you enter the soil beneath you. Feel any change in your body as you connect your energy into the Earth. In your mind's eye, see the image of the Tree of Life, a tree with branches reaching upwards balanced by roots reaching downwards. Impose this image over yourself until you become the Tree of Life. Your body is the trunk, your energetic branches reach into the energy space around and above your head, and the energy you reach downwards into the Earth is your roots. Breathe for a few moments as a great tree, connecting Earth with body and sky. Breathe, and trust whatever feelings arise. You are rooted to the Earth. What do your roots feel as they reach into the soil?

Does it feel good to be rooted, or do you feel stuck in one place? Can you gently open your energetic roots to the nourishment of the Earth? Allow yourself to connect deeply to the ground beneath you. When you are finished, pull your energy back into your body but stay connected by a few strands with the Earth to keep you grounded. Breathe, and come into your normal senses.

CRAFT

PINCH POT
TEALIGHT HOLDER

Peaceful lighting is key when setting the tone for an evening of self-care. Picture taking a bath surrounded by the warm glow of candles dancing in your newly made tealight holders, perhaps indulging in your favourite book or podcast – the perfect way to escape the busyness of everyday life and create your own contemplative bubble.

The repetitive process of creating light holes is, by its very nature, calming and therapeutic – an ideal task to focus a busy mind. You don't even need to own any specialist clay tools; you can use anything around the house to make your holes – why not try keys or the end of a spoon? You will be surprised by how the most unlikely of domestic objects can create interesting and unique shapes.

MAKES 2

TOOLS AND MATERIALS

· scissors
· 400g (14oz) white air-drying clay (see pages 52–53)
· clingfilm (plastic wrap)
· knitting needle
· small glass of water
· fine sandpaper

METHOD

1. Using the scissos, cut the clay in half, then wrap one half in clingfilm (plastic wrap) and leave to use another time.

2. Roll the other half into a ball using your hands. Try not to work the clay too much, as this will dry it out and cracks will appear.

3. Poke your thumb into the middle of the ball, stopping about two-thirds of the way down the pot.

4. Holding the pot in the palm of your hand, start to enlarge the hole in the middle by gently pressing the sides of the clay between your thumb and two fingers. Work your way around the hole, turning the pot as you work, so that you get an even thickness of clay wall all the way around. Keep enlarging the hole until the sides of your pot are 5mm–1cm (¼–½in) thick.

5. Place the pot on a flat surface and gently press down on the base to flatten it.

6. If the rim of the pot is slightly uneven and wonky, you can trim it with a sharp pair of scissors. Smooth out any rough edges using a dab of water and your finger.

7. Next, make a number of holes around the sides of your pot for the light to shine through. To create these, pierce through the clay with a knitting needle, holding the inside of the pot with your other hand so that it doesn't collapse under the pressure. Once your pots are dry, smooth any rough edges using fine sandpaper

FEEL THE MOMENT,
BREATHE, THEN MOVE ON
TO THE NEXT

THREADS OF CONNECTION

The wish for happiness is something that all living beings share. This is our common personal goal, and so many of the things we do from day-to-day in our lives have this intention behind them, even if they might seem quite unrelated. Becoming aware of our collective desire for happiness enables us to perhaps see a little more through the eyes of another. We can understand, for example, that if anger or fear arise in someone, this may be because a protective instinct has been triggered, which is an expression of a personal wish to be safe and therefore, at some level, a desire to maintain happiness.

Seeing this drive towards happiness as not just a personal but also a shared intent, can help us to identify with, rather than feel alienated by, someone whose behaviour may be very different from our own. This is not always easy, and it may require us to explore a person's backstory to really be able to see things from their perspective, but it is a brave step in the direction of generating more compassion in the way we see others.

We are all daughters and sons. Knowing that all of us are daughters or sons and have been born to a mother reinforces this sense of human connectedness.

CULTIVATING KINDNESS

Our connectedness as human beings can be directly experienced if we focus our meditation on compassion. But in the day to day, cultivating kindness doesn't always feel easy. It can be humbling to spot how many times we might fumble through an interaction with someone, intent on getting a task done successfully rather that bringing our open hearts to the fore, making eye contact and wishing them well as we go on our way. Making the effort to keep developing kindness towards all beings is a life-long undertaking. It is helpful to remember, though, how powerful it can be to show your care for the wellbeing of those you meet. Through us, the influence of kindness can spread its ripples wider, touching the lives of our children, families and communities, and helping to bring this simple attitude of care into the wider world. Take a moment to breathe and feel your connection to all life. Send some love to yourself and to all those around you.

MAKE A CREATIVE CHANGE

Use this creative exercise to switch up your thinking.

Pick something routine that you do every day, for example, walking the dog, making a cup of tea, checking your emails. Write a couple of sentences about this.

Now imagine that you have the outline for the next big blockbuster movie in front of you. It's up to you to come up with an exciting billboard poster with a caption to sell it. For example, on making a brew you might say, 'It was an ordinary day, an ordinary girl, but a steamy encounter was about to change everything!' Be creative and let your mind wander. You can draw your ideas or create the vision in your head.

When you spend a few minutes thinking creatively about everyday scenarios your perspective shifts. You see the wonder in the world and flex your imagination. It also puts you in a positive frame of mind.

A RITUAL FOR PATIENCE AND WISDOM

Develop a deep well of patience and wisdom with this easy ritual.

If you have a garden, find a patch of soil and sit beside it. If not, you can use a plant pot filled with soil. You will also need some seeds of your choice.

Close your eyes and take a few deep breaths. Imagine a beam of light travelling down from the sky, hitting the top of your head and surging through you. Picture this light flowing into your hands and along your fingertips, infusing you with creative energy. Open your eyes and dip the fingers of both hands deep into the soil. Sift the earth rhythmically through your fingers, as if you're adding air to this earthy mixture. As you do this repeat the chant, 'I am at one with the universe and part of a much bigger picture.' Sow the seeds, then cover lightly with the soil. To finish, water them, and as you do this say, 'My patience grows, like the seeds I sow.'

The physical activity of sowing and then nurturing the seeds re-enforces the idea that you also nurture qualities like patience and understanding. This, combined with a powerful affirmation that is repeated when the seeds are watered, helps to reprogram the way you think and feel.

There is no rush.

*Everything happens at
the right time for me.*

Patience fills my soul.

*My inner wisdom grows
with every breath.*

THE MAGIC OF BIRDSONG

Of all the species of bird in our forests and woodlands, savannahs and wetlands, it was the songbirds, the passerines, which emerged from their branch of the evolutionary tree most recently. How lovely for human beings that this should be so. We have the full-throated nightingale and the thrush, the mockingbird and the lark ascending, all singing lustily in our time: our era on Earth is enhanced by their song. Many a poet has been moved to write of an individual bird – Walt Whitman, Keats and others.

One aspect of learning how to live mindfully is to learn how to listen.

TUNE INTO NATURE

Learning to listen can have a similar effect. The birdwatcher out in the natural world is well placed to explore this area of experience. It may entail shutting our eyes for a few minutes, or, while walking, switching attention from the windows of our eyes, to focus on what we can hear. Farmyard sounds from the distance may come to our ears, the drone of a high-flying aeroplane, someone chopping wood, the wind in the trees, the barking of a dog, the patter of approaching rain. Best of all is birdsong, both close at hand and remote: a lark carolling from on high can be deeply moving. Much of the time we shut out all these sounds.

The call and song of birds is a great undeserved gift; become acquainted with it and we open up a new approach to bird identification. Often it will be the bird call or a snippet of song that reveals the identity of the singer. There is a useful app for this that can be downloaded to a mobile phone – although personally I prefer to linger and listen long enough to build up my own inner reference system. Once you have identified a bird by its song by yourself, it is hard to forget. It becomes an alternative way of knowing.

APRIL

*Time to connect. Make music,
listen to birdsong – and each
other – and just be present.*

THE FEATHER

Find a feather; hold it in your hand, blow on it and let it drop: watch as it floats in the air. So light! The feather, unique to birds, is a miracle of efficient design. Take a moment to appreciate the mystery of such a wonderful creation.

The creative evolution that made the feather is truly remarkable. Human technology could not have devised anything better. As we contemplate this natural phenomenon, we become mindful of the fact that we live our lives immersed in a living mystery; we are just one branch of the extraordinary emergence of life on the planet.

IN PRAISE OF COLOUR

The spring plumage of birds, males resplendent in their courting colours, is well recognized, and anticipated, amongst birdwatchers. We learn to identify birds in their states of dress both before and after their annual moult. But the bright new colours of spring are not always the result of new growth. The male redstart, for example, looks very different and much less distinguished in the summer months, and it is only when the ends of his throat and breast feathers become worn away during winter that they reveal the lovely black throat and rich rufous breast of spring. It is a glorious change brought about through wear.

Many of the more colourful feathers that have evolved in nature, from egrets to eagles, jays to orioles, pheasants to exotic birds of paradise, are so beautiful that they became the chosen adornments for a new arrival on the evolutionary scene: human beings, with their penchant for fashionable hats and headdresses. The emblematic tail of the peacock (actually covet feathers – the true, rather ordinary tail lies beneath) with its rich greens and blues, startling eye patterns and fan-like display, is an extravagant example of how far nature will go in supplying birds with an advantageous means of competition in courtship.

NATURE

IRIDESCENCE

A wonderful variety in the patterning of colour helps to identify the owner of a feather found on the ground; variegated or vermiculated, barred or plain, all are arrestingly beautiful, each in its own way. But there is one form of feather colour that catches the eye in a particularly startling manner: iridescence. We witness this only when it is presented to us from a particular angle: subtly on the necks of some pigeons, vividly on the backs and wings of many species of glossy starling in Africa, and memorably from the throats, cheeks and crowns of many hummingbirds.

Nature creates colour in feathers through colour pigments. Black pigment is especially robust and appears in the wing tips of many birds, protecting them from wear. Iridescence, however, is created by fine ribbing on the surface of the feather, which breaks up the wavelengths of light, reflecting them selectively. We have a sense that the bird is signalling to us as we watch. By observing the bird we help create what we see; without an observer the colours would be missed.

MOVEMENT

DANCER'S POSE

Natarajasana

DURATION: 2–3 minutes
YOGA STYLE: Iyengar yoga
GOOD FOR: Improving balance and focus

Begin in Mountain Pose. Shift your weight onto your right leg and firm your core. Inhale, lift your left foot behind you and catch hold of the outside edge of the foot with your left hand. Bring your knees together and extend your right arm parallel to the floor, palm facing down. Exhale, press the foot back into your hand and lift it to bring the thigh parallel to the floor. Keep your hips square; don't let the left hip lift. Reach forwards as your torso hinges and the left foot rises above your head. To exit, bring the left knee to the right and lower the foot and arm. Repeat on the left.

Hold the poses for 10–15 breaths. As you practise, visualize an emerald ray emanating from the centre of your chest. Feel this energy opening your heart and enabling you to dive into the pool of emotional strength, infinite love, deep empathy and radical forgiveness.

MODIFICATIONS

For balance, lightly touch your front hand on a wall or the back of a chair.

VARIATION: FOOT CLASP (INTERMEDIATE)

Once in the pose, bring the front arm back and clasp the inner foot.

1. MOUNTAIN POSE

2. DANCER'S POSE

EMBRACING THANKFULNESS

Blessing our food at mealtimes is an expression of thankfulness that happens the world over. It is something that we do when we are able to take a moment for conscientious reflection, often if we are part of a group, if a particularly special or large meal has been prepared, or if we ourselves are taking time to cook attentively. It doesn't seem automatic or habitual; rather, after a long morning of cooking, the moment of blessing is an opportunity to stand back and reflect on what has been achieved and thank all those involved: from gardeners, cooks, goats, chickens, cows and earthworms. It is a moment of putting everything into perspective and enjoying a quietness as we stand looking at the food we have created together. When we bless our food, we are voicing our appreciation of how lucky we are to be part of this continuum, we are acknowledging that others may not be so lucky, which makes us all the more grateful.

*Food is energy for my
mind, body and soul.*

*I am thankful for the food
that is on my plate.*

*I appreciate the
nourishment and the
enjoyment that this meal
brings and the people
I can share it with.*

URSA MAJOR

LATIN FOR: *Larger or Great Bear*

The Big Dipper is commonly thought of as a constellation, but it is
in fact an asterism (a pattern of stars) within the constellation of
Ursa Major. The seven stars – Alkaid, Mizar, Alioth, Megrez, Phecda,
Merak and Dubhe – actually form part of the back and tail of the bear,
commonly thought of as female.

To make out the rest of the bear you'll need a dark sky, as the other
stars are much fainter. The Big Dipper is commonly known as the
Plough in the UK and Ireland, and the Großer Wagen ('Great Wagon')
in Germany. The Big Dipper has been an important navigation tool for
centuries. One of the first facts you might have learnt about the night
sky is that the outer edge of the Big Dipper's 'bowl' leads you to Polaris,

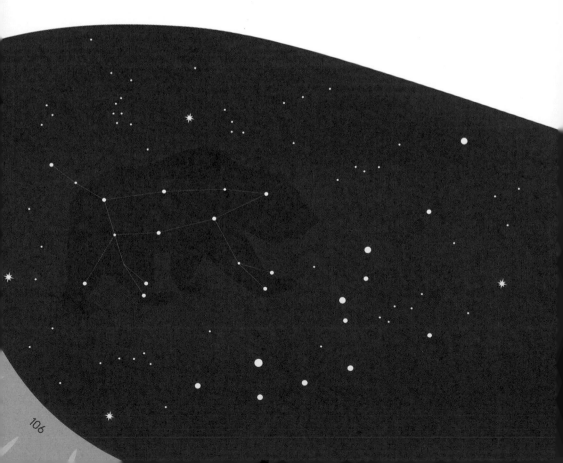

the North Star: extend the imaginary line that runs between the stars of Merak and Dubhe up into the sky and, at about five times the distance between these two stars, you'll find Polaris and hence magnetic north.

A VIEW THAT CONNECTS ALL OF HUMANITY

When we look up at the night sky, there is no other view in our human experience that we can share with so many others through time. Landscapes have changed over the millennia but the night sky has remained more or less the same. The Ursa Major constellation's association with a bear is testament to this – it's a connection that must have formed many millennia ago, before humans spread out from Eurasia and into North America. Thousands of years ago, people looked up at the night sky, just like we do today, and saw a wild animal in the heavens. We may appear separated by time or geography, but when it comes down to it, we're all just humans.

SOIL

Though we call it 'dirt', and refer to something impure as 'soiled', we depend on the complex matrix that is soil for our lives. Plants can be grown in controlled conditions in water, but most of the food we eat, and virtually all of the oxygen-producing land plants, grow in soil. Black, humusy soil; thick, red clay; dusty, light-brown silt – soil varies immensely, depending on where you are and how it was formed.

You can smell some of its history simply by scooping up a handful of earth. Metals and rocks smell tangy and dusty, while the sweet smell of organic matter comes from certain kinds of bacteria. Bits of decaying organic matter like shredded leaves smell like the wet and mossy forest floor. Threads of fungus give off a mushroomy smell. Soil that has sat untouched and too wet can give off an unpleasant decaying smell, which comes from the lack of oxygen. What does the scent of your own garden soil tell you about your land and climate? What images or associations spring to mind when you take a deep whiff of your soil?

We can deepen our understanding of the process of gardening by looking into the network of relationships that makes up the soil. It isn't just dirt, but a fluctuating dance of microbes, bugs, minerals, plants and even ourselves. Understanding and cultivating this relationship consciously, we enter into our own rich darkness.

Touch, smell and maybe even taste the soil, and your body sinks a little deeper into the groundedness of the garden. We sense more deeply the complexity of life, the dynamism of soil and gut and decay that all lead to growth and life.

Not just the yin and the yang, but the swirl and flow between these poles, the strands of the web of relationship that is a garden.

NATURE

MAKING NATURAL SEEDBOMBS

There are many different recipes for making seedbombs and experimenting is part of the fun! Seedbombs are like miniature gardens – they will be the first soil the seedlings grow in and they need to supply nutrients and have good drainage, like a full-blown garden. They can bring folliage and flowers to urban landscapes or neglected areas which in turn encourages pollinators to the environment.

Some people make their own garden compost from household waste such as vegetable peelings and garden trimmings. Others buy it from the local garden centre, or dig earth out of their gardens.

Some seedbomb recipes are simply soggy compost and seeds compressed to make a ball, but these tend to break up in the air or on landing, leaving the seeds much more vulnerable.

It is best to use something to bind the seedbomb and make it hard enough to survive impact with the ground. Whatever you use needs to be water–soluble also, so that water can infiltrate the seedbomb, get to the seeds and break their dormancy.

Some recipes use paper pulp made from egg boxes and office stationery waste that has been mixed with compost. As the paper dries, it binds everything together.

Additions such as fertilizers, secondhand tea leaves and coffee grounds provide nutrients to boost the germination process and promote vigorous plant growth.

How much seed you use depends on the size of the seed; for example, the bigger the seed, the more compost and clay you'll need to add to the mixture and the bigger the bomb will need to be in order to accommodate them.

Be generous but not wasteful, because too many seeds will result in overcrowding and bad air circulation, which can make the plants suffer from fungal diseases such as stem rot.

Follow the recipe on pages 112–113 to make your own seedbombs.

NATURE

SEEDBOMBS

This seedbomb recipe uses natural ingredients – compost and clay. The compost offers nutrients for the seeds to germinate and grow strong during their infancy, and the clay binds the seedbomb, making it hard enough not to break when it hits the ground.

MAKES 6

INGREDIENTS

- 5 tbsp of seed compost
- 4 tbsp of terracotta clay powder
- 1 tsp of seeds (note: base this on poppy seeds as a size guide and add half a tsp more as the seeds go up in size)
- 1 tsp of chilli powder as a pest deterrent (optional)
- 20ml/^{2}/$_3$fl oz water
- Liquid fertilizer (if NPK is absent in the compost)

EQUIPMENT

- a bowl
- a strong spoon
- kitchen paper or egg box
- an apron (optional)

TIP
When rolling your seedbombs, keep your palms flat to get a rounder shape. If your palms are slightly cupped, you get a shape not unlike a spinning top. Use your fingers to adjust the shape until you are happy with it.

METHOD

1. Pour the compost into the bowl.

2. Add the clay powder, seeds and chilli powder, if using.

3. Stir the dry ingredients together until well mixed.

4. Add the water in small amounts at a time, mixing, until you form a dough-like consistency that sticks together nicely (not too sticky and not too dry).

5. Divide the mixture into six even portions.

6. Roll each portion into a smooth ball.

7. Place the finished seedbombs on something absorbent, like kitchen paper or an egg box, and leave to dry for 2–48 hours, so that they keep their shape.

HOW TO USE

Launch the seedbombs once they have set (if it is the right time of year); they will germinate quicker because they are still moist.

Alternatively, they can be stored for up to two years and beyond, though some seeds may not germinate if left too long, especially vegetables. The seeds will remain dormant until activated by water.

GOING BACK

Our lives are the source of rich material, and it's well worth delving into them to find gems for enriching our writing. Some of us might consider our own lives to have been rather mundane, too ordinary to be of interest to readers. But every life is full of wonder. There have been people, places, and experiences we've known which have all had their fascination for us, and we only need to convey this in our writing for readers to be equally fascinated. When we practise expressing in words the full impression of our memories, we are developing skills that will strengthen the power of our writing.

Many people want to write their life story for their family to read, but it can also be a rewarding exercise in itself.

Our lives can be treated like fictional stories, introducing 'bookmarks' that crop up from time to time and provide structure to the writing. We will return to the concerns of our childhood and our teenage years, trying to recall how it felt to be so young. We'll remember how important our pleasures and worries felt to us then, although we might since have dismissed them as trivial.

We'll also revisit the people we have known in our lives: people we haven't seen for years, people who shaped our lives, and others we live with every day. After all, our life story is not just the past, it is also the present, and what we choose to write about now.

BOOKMARKS

Writing about our own lives is a great way of developing writing skills. But writing a whole life story raises the question of what to include and what to leave out. We owe it to ourselves as writers to make it an interesting read. So, as with any narrative, our story needs shape and structure. Structure can be provided in a life story by consciously including points of interest, or 'narrative bookmarks' that occur and reoccur throughout and hold the reader's attention. These bookmarks could concern particular interests and activities, family, travel, health or career. Taking one or more of these into account creates a pattern for your story. It will give perspective to chronological events, description of personalities, accounts of schooling, career and more. The bookmarks might have their own narrative too, as an interest becomes a career, a problem is overcome, an ambition is realized.

Write a list of 'bookmarks' that have occurred and reoccurred in your own life. These may evoke happy memories, difficult ones, or both. Be specific: for example, write 'brain surgeon' or 'sales assistant' rather than 'my job'. Don't give it too much thought; you will not need to use them all, and writing a list quickly can help to include useful ideas that wouldn't occur with too much overthinking.

NOURISHING THE DANCE OF LIFE

When we nestle a tiny seed into the soil, we plant a prayer. We ask the soil to protect and nourish this seed of life. Then we wave our magic wand – the kind that water comes out of – and whisper a spell that sets off a series of relationships that will eventually lead to a salad or a soup gracing our table. We pray: grow. The soil wraps its damp darkness around this little seed, this promise, and when the seed bursts its skin and reaches out with a tiny root filament, the soil says yes. The roots grasp on to tiny particles of sand and stone, and the soil hugs back. It affirms the life of the sprout, holding it in place and time. It gently feeds it nutrients and water in just the right amount. Slowly the sprout turns into a seedling, then a plant, eventually producing a fruit. All of this growth is supported by the soil tucked around its roots.

We nourish the dance of life when we build garden soil. Adding compost, manure, minerals and other amendments feeds the network of bacteria, fungi, nematodes and earthworms. Eventually, this care will resonate into macro communities as the soil feeds plants and the plants feed animals, including us humans.

The nourished soil, together with the ancient minerals present since before life began on Earth, feeds that seed you planted. It holds and nourishes it like a mother holding her child. As the child of the Earth, the plant grows bigger and stronger, it reaches deep down inside this support network. Only with strong support is it able to also stand tall and reach into the sky, like a dancer, strong and lithe. Eventually, the plant is ready to gift itself to the flow of life.

When you pull a carrot from the soil, dust off the earth and hand it to your neighbour, you are participating in the vast strands of life that begin in the soil.

Perhaps we, too, feel a similar support when we participate in this dance. The soil holds us. It literally holds our weight. It nourishes our food, which in turn nourishes our bodies. It accepts what we give it, and gives us back the gift of green and growing things. Because of the complex darkness of living soil, we have shade from the oak, the sweetness of strawberries and even each breath of fresh air. And when our journey is complete, the cells that make up our bodies will return to the soil, eventually gifting our nourishment to the cycle of life.

CRAFT

WOODEN LETTER OPENER

This wooden letter opener is a simple double-edged knife tapering to a sharp tip. Thin knife-shaped tools are invaluable around the house. Whether whittling a makeshift palette knife for mixing glue or a kitchen implement for scraping, or spreading or serving, it is often the case that a short, flat wooden tool is just what you need for the job. A letter opener reminds you of how nice it is to receive handwritten letters. Once you have made your letter opener, why not write a letter to a friend or loved one?

MAKES 1

TOOLS AND MATERIALS

- Slöjd knife
- Thin rectangular billet such as field maple, approx. 2.5 x 1.2 x 18cm (1 x ½ x 7in)
- Pencil
- Card (optional)

METHOD

1. Using the knife, clean up the wood and ensure it has smooth, straight surfaces. Using a pencil mark out a curved edge tapering to a point at one end. For symmetry, you could make a template using a piece of folded card so that each side mirrors the other. Carve the tapered shape, leaving the edges thick and square.

2. To create a sharp edge on either side of the letter opener's blade, carve a pair of facets or bevels on each side of the blade. Draw a centre line down the length of the blade, using a concave cut to blend in to where the blade meets the handle. Working from the handle towards the tip of the blade, carve each of the bevels.

3. Continue carving the bevels, aiming for thin, sharp edges and a crisp central line. Try to create symmetrical curves at the handle end, to blend the handle into the blade in an attractive way.

4. Carefully remove the square edges along each side of the rectangular handle.

5. Chamfer the end of the handle by removing the sharp edges using small cuts.

MEDITATION

MINDFULNESS AS A HABIT

The phrase 'a force of habit' refers to the inherent momentum that a habit has. A regular routine pulls us into its familiarity, building a weight of its own over time. The routines we set and keep for ourselves eventually become automatic habits, and that includes intentional planned practices of mindfulness.

We will naturally create for ourselves habits and routines. But with the self-awareness that comes with mindfulness, we can be more intentional about the way we form our habits and routines, to better support us in our scholarly practices, and nourish us along the way. The routines that are already there in our day can become powerfully calming if we use them to still our minds and be fully present. These moments can be the pauses that punctuate the daily grind and create little windows for us to look within ourselves.

RITUAL

THE MAGIC OF RITUALS

Just as our routines over time become habits, so too can our habits become rituals, if they are done mindfully and solemnly, with a sense of reverence and slowness. Daily rituals are like the cool, smooth stepping-stones that we rest on as we navigate through our busy days – micro-events of magic that we look forward to, which create a sense of calm and grounding to our days and weeks.

We can make ritual out of any mundane task if it is done with a mindset to make it special. All we need do is bring our present awareness to our actions, ourselves and the space and objects around us, and pay attention as though we are savouring a rare delight. This might be catching the sunshine on your yoga mat for a few stretches to tune into yourself. Or making a chai and taking it outside to drink, inhaling its spiced scent, feeling the warmth of it emanating to your hands from the ceramic cup, sipping it slowly as you watch the breeze dancing and swaying through the trees.

*When used
to break up a long,
labourius task, our
moments of mindfulness
can nurture us and soothe
our souls.*

GREETING THE SUNRISE

Rise early, very early, while it is still dark, and we can witness one of the great wonders of the natural world: the dawn chorus. After a break without eating, often huddled against the cold, birds wake and burst into song as they greet the sunrise. In town and countryside, they proclaim the day from treetop and chimney pot, in woodland and open field, particularly in the spring. The volume of sound can be quite astonishing. And as the birdwatcher knows, the early morning can be the best time for observing, when the birds are up and about feeding.

In Native American mythology, the dawn chorus has long been recognized as a special event. The Jicarilla Apache creation myth recounts how the most powerful of the spiritual beings, Black Hactcin, after making the animals, created the first bird by mixing soil with a drop of rain. This pleased Black Hactcin, so deciding that the bird needed companions, he grabbed it by its feet and whirled it around in a clockwise direction until it became dizzy, its head filled with strange images and dreamlike forms. When the bird recovered, the dreams had taken shape, and there they all were – eagles and sparrows, hawks and herons, hummingbirds, swifts and crows.

The birds quickly became anxious that one day Black Hactcin would leave them, so they asked for a companion to care for them, a human being. Black Hactcin agreed to the request and sent the birds and animals out foraging for all the materials needed: white clay, black jet, red stone, opal, red ochre and dark clouds for hair. He then marked an outline on the ground, an outline like himself, and put all the gathered materials into it. He summoned the wind to enter the moulded form and the wind left whorls on the fingertips where it entered the body.

While this magic was happening, the Black Hactcin had commanded the birds and animals not to look – but the birds, in twittering excitement, could not resist the temptation and did look, causing the magic to go slightly awry (which is why some of us appear a bit odd!). Nevertheless, they all burst into exuberant song when the first human came alive, as they still do every morning with the dawn chorus.

MAY

Time to be. Picnics, sunshine and magical skies mark meaningful experiences ready to be created.

MINDFULNESS FOR THE INFORMATION AGE

TECHNOLOGY AS OUR FRIEND

We need to be aware of the possible negative side-effects of our information age. But we can also make use of technology to help us be more mindful.

Research has shown that between 2000 and 2015 the average Westerner's attention span dropped from 12 seconds to 8 seconds. This is where mindfulness can really help. When we meditate and rest our attention on something, we notice every time this attention drifts off and we bring it back. In this way, mindfulness is actually a practice for training our concentration skills.

Zen master Thich Nhat Hanh advocated setting an alarm every 15 minutes to remind you to come into the moment. There is now a whole range of guided meditation apps that give access to recordings from many teachers and record how many minutes you have meditated. Other wearable technology allows you to track your breathing patterns through the day, your heart rate and heart rate variability (a measure of your state of calm). All these tools can help us be more mindful if used in the right way.

The next time your phone pings, notice the compulsion to check it. Be aware of how your hand automatically moves to your pocket. Notice that impatient yearning to know who is contacting you. Where do you feel it most in the body? How do these feelings change as you stay with them, without looking at your phone? Use that ping as a reminder to reconnect to the moment.

SEATED TWIST

Ardha Matsyendrasana

DURATION: 2–3 minutes
YOGA STYLE: Classical Hatha
GOOD FOR: Restorative

Begin seated, legs bent, feet flat on the floor. Bring the left foot under the right leg with the heel next to the right hip. Step the right sole to the mat by the outer left thigh. Inhale, lengthen your spine and place your right hand lightly on the mat behind you. Exhale and twist to the right, wrapping your left arm around your knee. Look over your right shoulder and ground through the right sitting bone. To exit, exhale and unwind back to centre. Release the legs and repeat on the left.

MODIFICATIONS

If your sitting bone lifts, straighten the underneath leg. Sit on a folded blanket to lengthen the spine.

VARIATION: BOUND TWIST (INTERMEDIATE)

Take the left arm around the outside of the right thigh and thread it through the gap. Bring the right arm around your back and clasp your hands, or use a strap to connect.

SEATED TWIST

REAL GRATITUDE

Gratitude can never be forced; there may be times when we know that we ought to be grateful, and may even express the thought in appropriate words, but inside we do not have the feeling. Our gratitude becomes no more than an act, a bit fake, while inside we are losing out and may find ourselves hoping that the acting will one day be replaced by something more worthy – a real, fulfilling sense of being grateful.

The natural world with all its rich beauty is a great giver and promoter of gratitude – so long as we are mindfully open to the opportunities it offers. The gift of gratitude is unbidden and wells up from within us with a feeling of joy and perhaps laughter. When this spiritual blessing comes to us we do well to welcome and foster it, recognizing that we have been given something good, and resolving to look for it in our lives more often. We can be grateful for feeling grateful.

SEEDBOMBS FOR BUTTERFLIES

Butterfly Conservation (butterfly-conservation.org) believes that butterflies and moths are a fundamental part of our heritage and are indicative of a healthy environment. It is important to grow food plants right through the season from when they come out of hibernation in spring to autumn, when they need to build up their energy reserves for winter. Using the seeds from butterfly-friendly varieties in seedbombs should generate plants that will provide hibernation, somewhere to lay eggs, food for the larvae (caterpillars) and nectar for butterflies.

Follow the recipe on pages 112–113 and use a combination of any of the seeds below to create a butterfly-friendly seedbomb.

BUTTERFLY-FRIENDLY PLANTS

- Foxglove *Digitalis purpurea*
- Red campion *Silene dioica*
- Ox-eye daisy *Leucanthemum vulgare*
- Lesser knapweed *Centaurea nigra*
- Field scabious *Knautia arvensis*
- Corn cockle *Agrostemma githago*

WILD CHAMOMILE
Matricaria chamomilla

Chamomile was cultivated as early as the Neolithic period and has been used for centuries as a 'cure-all' medicinal plant. A great companion plant, as its strong, aromatic flowers attract beneficial insects that feed on pest predators, such as aphids. May is the perfect month to launch or plant chamomile seeds.

STEMS Branched, upright, smooth stem.

LEAVES The long and narrow alternate leaves can be harvested fresh from the plant for medicinal uses.

FLOWERS Yellow and comb-like centres, surrounded by 10–20 white petals. Harvest the flowers for medicinal uses when open and fresh or dry for later use. It takes 20–35 days from flower to seed.

SEEDS 1mm ($^1/_{25}$in) elongated, light brown and ridged.

LAUNCH SEEDBOMBS April–May and August–September.

GERMINATION TIME 1–2 weeks.

HARVESTING SEEDS Seeds ripen July to September.

PLANT CARE Don't cut back the foliage before flowering as the flower production will reduce dramatically. To remove aphids wash off with a strong jet of water.

PESTS AND DISEASES Can suffer aphid attacks, which attract hungry ladybirds. Generally disease-free but susceptible to rust, downy mildew and powdery mildew.

CULINARY AND MEDICINAL USES Chamomile has soothing properties and is used to help alleviate conditions such as nervousness, anxiety, hysteria, headaches, stomach pains, indigestion, colds and flu. Also used as a poultice for swellings, sprains and bruises. Steep for 15 minutes then drink for a gentle sleep aid.

FAMILY Asteraceae/Compositae

NATIVE TO Southern Europe

HEIGHT/SPREAD 60 x 40cm (23⅝ x 15¾in)

HABITAT Roadsides, railways, waste ground, fields, arable land

THRIVES IN Full sun/partial shade

SOIL Most soil types; tolerates poor soils

LIFESPAN Annual

FLOWERS May–August

FORM Upright

LEAF FORM Upper: Bipinnate; Lower: Tripinnate

POLLINATED BY Insects

POLARIS

LATIN FOR: *The Pole Star*

The star Polaris, located at the end of the Ursa Minor ('Smaller Bear') constellation, lies nearly in a direct line with the Earth's rotational axis, marking the North Celestial Pole and making it the pole star of the Northern Hemisphere.

We all need a polestar, a navigation point that remains still amongst the whirlwind of life. That point may be our home, a partner, an old friend, a spiritual teacher or a book. We often don't realize how important our polestar is until it's lost or uprooted. In periods of great change in our life, such as bereavement, divorce, or moving home, we need that anchor holding us steady as the waves crash all around us.

Without it, we have no fixed point of reference, no emotional compass, no stability. Take a moment to appreciate who or what in your life acts as your polestar, and how they or it has helped you through the years to weather the storms of life.

AN EVENING PERFORMANCE

We should always keep an eye out for the pre-sunset behaviour of birds: there is a lot happening as they prepare for the night, finding a safe roost, catching a last snack before hours of forced fasting, sorting out a refuge from bad weather. Some behaviour may come as a surprise: on a winter walk in Europe we might come upon a large flock of female chaffinches in a thorn bush, all facing west as their fluffed-up feathers absorb the last rays of the setting sun, sharing a communal need to get warm before dark.

The flocking of starlings in the evening has become well known, as hundreds of thousands of birds – a great 'murmuration' – sweep and dance about the sunset sky in close formation. They become as one, a blob of darkness mysteriously held together as though by telepathy – a living, shape-shifting, amoeba-like being, twisting and turning at great speed in unison in the fading light. Why they do it and how they accomplish their aerodynamics remains something of a mystery at which we can only marvel. And then suddenly, as if in response to a hidden instruction, the show comes to an end and the birds fall out of the sky, funnelling down to roost noisily in a reed bed or beneath a seaside pier.

Wherever you happen to live there will be something to look out for, a
local evening performance, as birds prepare for the night. If you live
near a river estuary then the evening sky will become a river of gulls
as they row lazily down to the sea for the night, their day of grubbing
for food in the fields over. In the autumn, in particular, they are joined
by gossiping skeins of Canada geese heading in the same direction,
aiming for the water meadows and mudflats where they can roost in
safety, away from foxes and other predators; there is safety in numbers.
In winter they are accompanied by other species of migratory goose
and many types of duck, so that the evening sky becomes a brief swirl
of activity. Black forms arrayed in purposeful formation silhouetted
against the sunset sky.

ART JOURNALS

Artists collect, interpret and reconfigure. As much as we might try, the enigma of what goes on within us throughout the creative process cannot be explained. Art journals can be a tool for us to bring awareness into our artistic practice. Just as in a puzzle, sometimes we don't know where all the parts of our practice fit or how it will come together. We just work diligently until we make sense of pieces and how they relate to one another. By keeping an art journal, we keep a record of these pieces as they come to us.

How often have we had wonderful ideas only for them to evaporate? Like dreams, such moments of inspiration can be ephemeral. Carrying or keeping a journal and adding notes, sketches and ideas each day is a way of mindfully tuning in to those moments that can otherwise slip away. When we write down or sketch these observations we can include details that we may not recall later. The act of recording such experiential flashes by hand makes them concrete in a way that snapping a photograph or trying to make a mental note of them won't.

JOURNAL AS ARTWORK

Art journals can also become something of an artwork in themselves.
They can relieve us of the pressure of a fresh white canvas and, as
such, end up forming an imperfect, unresolved artistic snapshot of
our methods, process and techniques, the experiments and sources
of inspiration, the slip ups and half-completed attempts. Each aspect of
what we engage with has its own artistry and together makes for
a fascinating and often beautiful creative item. Some artists focus solely
on the creation of art journals as their artistic product.

Anything can go into a journal, and for this reason it can open you up
to using processes and materials that you might never have previously
considered. Perhaps you might collage bits of sketches you did on
napkins in a café, or tear something out of a newspaper or magazine.
Use your morning coffee dregs and push them around with your finger.
Add textures onto your pages by laying them down and rubbing them
to create embossing. Make little origami cranes with bus ticket stubs
and collect them in an envelope at the back of your journal. The more
you embrace journalling, the more you will find yourself creating and
playing with the world around you.

HELLO RAINBOW

When you're feeling stressed and need to calm down and distance yourself from a situation, try this on-the-spot visualization.

To begin, find an image of a rainbow and focus on it for a couple of minutes. When you're ready, close your eyes and imagine you're sitting beneath the arch of the rainbow in your picture. You can feel the warmth of the sun on the top of your head, infusing you with peace.

With every breath in and out, the rainbow extends, its colours spreading and becoming more vibrant. Continue to breathe deeply, and picture the rainbow gradually descending from the sky, until it's touching your head. Slowly it wraps around you, covering you from head to toe in an array of vivid hues. You are drenched in all the colours of the rainbow. When you inhale, you take in the uplifting energy of each ray. As you exhale you release all the fear, worry and stress back into the air.

When you are ready, emerge from the rainbow, give your limbs a shake and do a mental check of your body. You should feel light, centred, calm and relaxed.

Slow, deep breathing calms the body and the mind, and is particularly powerful when coupled with a visualization using colour and light.

I hold serenity in my soul.

I am cocooned in a rainbow of light.

Calmness covers me.

I soar above the stress.

LEAVES

Leaves are elegantly crafted into many different shapes and sizes with the primary goal of harvesting light. They must be sheetlike, thin and translucent (to allow light to reach the innermost cells). They must have stalks, which may develop in an opposite or alternate pattern on the stem and elevate the leaves to positions where they can track the movement of the sun throughout the day.

There is an unlimited diversity in leaf characteristics. Some come in single blades or are divided into leaflets; some have leaf margins, which can be whole, toothed or wavy. All these characteristics are what botanists use to identify and describe a plant. Below are just some examples of leaf shapes and patterns found in nature. Why not go for a walk in a local park and see how many you can spot. Focus on the detail of the leaves you notice, appreciating the differences and similarities of each one.

OPPOSITE   **ALTERNATE**   **PINNATE**

DISSECTED

HEART-SHAPED

OBLIQUE

OBLANCEOLATE

LANCEOLATE

OBLONG

PALMATE

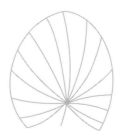

ROUND

SUNSET WONDERS

There is an ebb and flow of life in the twilight skies of evening. The swallows and martins make their final forays for insects in the fading light, dashing hither and thither; the screaming swifts cleave the air for the last time before nightfall. No sooner have the birds gone to rest, roosting in their nests or on wires, or sleeping on the wing if they are swifts, then the darkening sky is inhabited again, this time by the night shift: by small flying mammals, bats, hunting for moths, mosquitoes and other insects that frequent the dark.

We – birds, bats and human beings – all share the same evening air, and yet how different are their worlds from ours. As we stand and breathe the evening and then night air, we become more deeply aware of the world we inhabit, astonished perhaps that we had no part to play in our own existence on the planet. We are here in the present moment and can only feel pleasure and gratitude.

MEDITATION

MINDFUL BREATHING

Find an ideal spot in your day's activity to practise this mindfulness breathing exercise. It is a well-tried and ancient practice, and is one of the simplest forms of meditation, accessible to everyone – the healthy and the sick, the old and the young, the troubled and the calm, the religious and the non-religious. Over two and a half thousand years ago, the buddha taught 'Right Mindfulness' (samma sati) to his followers as the seventh element of the Eightfold Path. He wanted them to wake up in this troublesome, transitory world and come to see things as they really are. To focus on one's breathing is to begin the process of enlightenment and growth in wisdom.

Sit with your feet square on the floor, your back straight (but not uncomfortably so), eyes relaxed and not searching about, but looking at whatever is in front of you. Then breathe in, slowly, naturally and a little deeper than usual. Feel the air filling your lungs; be aware of your body's need of it and its enlivening oxygen, and hold it there for a moment without any strain. Now breathe out as slowly as comes easily. Repeat several times, as many as you need, your attention focussed on the ingoing and outgoing breath. Quietly dismiss all other thoughts – tell them to come back later. Here you are, now, in this present moment, content to be where you are, enjoying nothing more than the life-giving breath as it flows in and out of your lungs.

PEOPLE

Let's go back and meet up with people you've known in your life. Maybe they are friends you played with as a child, or old pals you still meet regularly. They could be family members you loved but who have died. They may be someone you didn't know well but who gave you encouragement or support that you've never forgotten.

When we think of the people we love, or who've shared activities with us, or been kind, or made us laugh, we rarely think of their appearance. This is a lesson for us when writing character. Appearance is not usually of great importance (although a particular quirk of clothing, for example, a red scarf or tweed jacket, can serve as a useful 'bookmark'). It's better if something more indicative of a person's personality is used to bring them to life. Perhaps they loved gardening, baking cakes or watching soaps on TV. Maybe their house was always full of flowers. They might have chattered a lot, or been generous with gifts or time. Maybe their smile lit up the room.

Make a list of ten people
who have meant a lot to you in
your life. Some could be from
the distant past, others could be
people you see often today.

SUMMER

JUNE

JULY

AUGUST

SUMMER PLAYLIST

· **The Sea** – Morcheeba

· **Summer Mornings** – Dawzee

· **Hey Saturday Sun** – Boards of Canada

· **Beautiful Blue Sky** – Ought

· **Babys** – Bon Iver

· **Les Fleurs** – Minnie Riperton

· **Sunny Road** – Emilíana Torrini

Sunshine, stillness and self-care are the only roots I need.

My kindness will ripple out into the world like the streams into the seas.

I give myself permission to feel at peace.

JUNE

Time to feel. Painting what we see and noticing how it makes us feel is art from the heart.

BEES: A CREATURE OF THE SUN

The bee is a creature not just of our home, the Earth, but also of the sun. The honeybee's waggle dance to her sisters communicates the location of nectar sources using the sun as a reference point. We might participate in bee perception when planning the garden, for we too orient our garden beds and rows to the sun. We notice where the shadows fall in winter, and in summer where we have areas of complete sun or part shade. The garden and the bee remind us that all life comes from the sun. The bee depends on the sun to warm things up enough for her to fly; the plant depends on the sun to make food for itself, the bees and us; and we depend on the sun to make the garden possible. No matter our climate or growing zone, we gardeners – and bees – are united in our attention and connection to the sun.

THE BEE COMMUNITY

Usually when we think of bees, the honeybee comes to mind. One reason for the honeybee's success on Earth – they evolved from wasps hundreds of millions of years ago and haven't changed much since – is her social nature. Her hive is a superorganism, made up of thousands of individuals. The hive cannot exist without its members, and the individuals cannot survive without the hive. This is true of us humans, too. We depend on each other just as bees do, though we readily get mired in our arguments of difference and forget our interdependence. Bees and the garden can gently bring us back into the reality of our interconnection and need for community. When we share extra produce with a neighbour or a food bank, attend a seed swap in the spring or can tomatoes with a group, we cultivate community that strengthens our bodies and souls. We are all of the one great hive.

THE YIN AND YANG OF BEES

The bee, not unlike us humans, is a creature of contradiction. She gently visits delicate flowers to gather sweet nectar in order to transform it into miraculous honey, yet she carries with her always the power to inflict pain. She invites us, therefore, to hold the dialectic of life and death, yin and yang. Nothing is ever totally what it seems. Even bee venom, which we usually think of as bad (bee stings are painful, and even fatal to those prone to anaphylaxis), has the potential to cure serious disease. Holding the dialectic invites us into the present moment, out of our labels and judgements, in observation of the unfolding of life. We let go of trying to control, and simply watch the bee making her rounds from blossom to blossom in search of the goodness of life. We slow down, and we breathe.

MINDFUL AWARENESS THROUGH CREATIVITY

Mindfulness of the body is not just for practitioners of yoga. Creating art can be a highly physical practice. As artists we use the muscles across the whole of our bodies, and sometimes for great lengths at a time. Our hands grip and hold, our fingers pinch and shape, our arms gesture and our eyes focus. There is a beautiful synchronicity of body movements engaged in the physicality of making art that often happens outside of our consciousness. By bringing a mindful awareness to our bodies we can enrich the artistic experience and hone our technique of making, and we can also move towards a permanent connectedness between mind and body; as we observe the interplay between the two, we can learn to influence and master this duality.

When we are 'in' our bodies, drawing present awareness to the physical lived experience, we are less likely to be in our minds. This anchoring effect of dwelling in our physical self is powerful in its potential to calm the nervous system and settle the mind, thereby diminishing stress and improving overall health.

TUNE IN TO YOUR BODY

The act of creating provides a wonderful opportunity to yoke our mind and body. When we create art, we have a wellspring of physical sensations to connect with and find pleasure in. Scanning your body by taking note of how it feels all the way from head to toe is a great way of tuning in. You might do this at set intervals, such as at the beginning, middle and end of a creative session, until it becomes an organic part of your practice. Heightening our awareness of the physical self is a simple act that only requires us to set the intention and remember to do so. The more we do it, the more we may find the body is a familiar place to 'be'.

The body senses rather than thinks. Sense perception possesses an autonomy and perfection of its own. When we tune into the feeling of making we can be led by the physical sensations of practice rather than cognitive decision-making. In the dynamic movement of making we may find a wonderful release of tension. While sinking deep into the sensation of our actions we can find an inner stillness. When working on a pottery wheel, the repetitive, subtle rhythmic motions of the clay turning on the wheel can be incredibly calming and centring. The echo of the experience might continue to run over your hands and mind for hours after finishing.

WALKING THE BUDDHIST PATH

Two and a half thousand years ago, the Buddha incorporated mindfulness into his teaching as a major element in the Eightfold Path and the perennial fight against ignorance. He encouraged his followers to become more attentive to their bodies, their feelings and their thoughts; to get to know and understand that bundle of worries that threatens to spoil life; to become more aware. He lived at a time of great change, when the old religions were being questioned, and taught a new spiritual way to explore life, one that was available to anyone, whatever their caste and whether they were religious or not.

An early image of the Buddha shows him sitting; one hand trails forwards and is in touch with the ground. The original story is that the Buddha made a vow in a previous life to achieve enlightenment; in touching the ground, he is calling the earth to bear witness to the vow. He is meditating, but that does not mean he is away somewhere in the mind palace of his own head – he is earthed like a lightning conductor to physical reality, to the moment in the material and spiritual world.

One well-trodden way to practise mindfulness is to go for a good walk and to follow the Buddha's simple advice:

'*When walking – just walk.*'

MARIGOLD
Calendula officinalis

Marigold has been valued for many centuries for its healing powers and is one of the earliest cultivated medicinal flowers. The latter part of its Latin name, 'officinalis', is the botanical term meaning 'used in the practice of medicine'. Marigold is still a popular garden plant to this day.

STEMS Marigold has stout, upright, angular branched stems, which are pale green and covered in fine hairs.

LEAVES Alternate light green, covered in fine hairs, with widely spaced teeth.

FLOWERS The orange daisy-like flowers grow from a crown-shaped head. As the flower dies, a circular seed head remains.

SEEDS The achene (seeds) are closely curled inwards in the middle of what was the flower head. They are light brown when dry; spiky, woody and around 5–10mm ($^3/_{16}$–$^3/_8$in long).

LAUNCH SEEDBOMBS March–April.

GERMINATION TIME 1–2 weeks.

HARVESTING SEEDS Seeds ripen August–November.

PLANT CARE To encourage bushiness and more flowers, pinch out the growing tips. Deadhead to prevent the plant from becoming invasive. Irrigate during dry periods.

PESTS AND DISEASES Suffers attacks from slugs and aphids. Susceptible to powdery mildew.

CULINARY AND MEDICINAL USES The petals can be used in an edible flower salad or as a garnish. Collect flower heads or petals, dry, then seal in an airtight container. Herbalists value marigold/calendula for its skin-healing properties and many lotions are made from it to help treat ailments such as nappy rash, eczema, sunburn, ulcers, chicken pox, shingles, athlete's foot, cuts and grazes and to soothe irritated nipples.

FAMILY Compositae/Asteraceae

NATIVE TO Europe

HEIGHT/SPREAD 30 x 20cm (12 x 7¾in)

HABITAT Roadsides, railways, arable land, cultivated beds

THRIVES IN Full sun/partial shade

SOIL Grows on most well-drained moist soils; tolerates poor soils

LIFESPAN Hardy perennial

FLOWERS May–October

FORM Upright

LEAF FORM Spatulate or oblanceolate

POLLINATED BY Bees

MEDITATION CREATES MINDFULNESS

Meditation is a specific practice for creating mindfulness, allowing us to have the moments of recollection that we may need in our daily life. The Ānāpānasati meditation (often translated as 'mindfulness of breathing') is a practice where we apply attention to the physical sensations of breathing, to create focus and calm amidst a broad awareness of our body, mind and feelings.

There are many different versions of this practice. A simple version is counting each exhalation until you reach ten, then beginning a new cycle afresh. You can choose a period of time that suits you, a few minutes, ten, fifteen or more, if you like.

It sounds simple, and in some ways it is, but it isn't always easy; on some days it will come naturally, and on others, your mind will wander before you reach a count of three. If you are stressed, busy or emotionally distracted your mind may wander around to many other things. That is normal, so try not to worry; it becomes more familiar and sometimes gets a little easier with practice. Remember to treat yourself kindly; try not to tell yourself 'I can't do this', even if it's difficult.

Learning to love yourself completely can take time. You may have a good regard for who you are and find it relatively easy to be kind in your thoughts and words, but more than likely, you have good days and bad days, and your sense of self fluctuates depending on what's going on in your life.

Our own thoughts and feelings can help or hurt us, but they can be subtle and it can require a gentle persistence to be aware of them. Creating a continuity of self-care helps to keep alive our intention to act with care and kindness towards ourselves.

THE SPIRITUAL REALM

There are moments in life when the spiritual dimension breaks through and stirs us strangely, and a bird can be as much the cause of it as any other aspect of nature. We may hear the song of a thrush one evening, the singer high on the uppermost branch of a tree, proclaiming nothing less than joy. It catches our attention and we feel an aching sense of beauty, our spirits lifted as we are transported into a realm of the sublime. We find ourselves standing still, drawn into reverent silence by this unexpected gift.

In such moments we experience a heightened awareness of the mystery of our own existence, here and now; we feel at one with the bird, the song and the evening. To be a conscious part of the scene, to be awake to such a meaningful spiritual reality, has a quality of the miraculous. The disturbing beauty of the thrush's song stirs in us deep questions about what it means to be human in the world we perceive around us.

WHAT IS THE TRUE REALITY?

It is not possible for us to be mindfully aware of the spiritual dimension of the world all of the time. It is a truth concealed from us in those everyday activities that absorb our lives, only to be revealed in special memorable moments – moments that we should learn to cherish.

THE CONFERENCE OF THE BIRDS

Every religion has its mystical branch, a perennial philosophy that delves deeper into the nature of being, into what it means to be me. In Islam it is the Sufis who took seriously the idea of a hidden spiritual reality lying within and behind what is familiar: they used the language of allegory to explore and explain their experience. A mysterious being, the Simorgh bird, figures prominently in the renowned twelfth-century poem of Farid ud-Din Attar, 'The Conference of the Birds'. In the poem, a pilgrimage is made by a large mixed flock of birds, led by a wise and ancient hoopoe. The Simorgh represents God and is the goal of the pilgrimage.

In the allegory, each bird represents the faults and weaknesses of human beings. The poem explores the excuses made by men and women who, while intending to seek a spiritual understanding of life, get bogged down in selfish concerns. The nightingale wants to stay with his beloved, the parrot is seduced by his own beauty, the falcon prefers to hunt from a royal wrist, the proud partridge cannot let go of his Self, 'that whirlpool where our lives are wrecked'. Eventually, after many adventures, a determined few reach the land of the fabulous Simorgh, where they come to a mysterious lake, and make a startling discovery. They look into the water and, seeing only their own reflections, realize that far from being a flock of separate companions as they had thought, that they together are the Simorgh – each an emanation of the One, the divine creator.

RHYMES AND REASON

We live in a world of sound and rhythm. Indeed, we rely on a regular, rhythmic heartbeat to keep us alive. It's no wonder we respond to the music of life and nature; the very planet we live on spins and circles the sun with beautiful regularity.

Many writers feel sensitive to the rhythm and shape in language. And this isn't only in poems and songs. Whether spoken or written, words put together with a sense of pace and form can have a powerful effect.

For any writer committed to developing their skills, an insight into the rhythms and patterns of language can be provided by poetry. Even those who prefer prose can benefit from spending time with poetry; it enhances our writing by guiding us to use the right tone and pace for the atmosphere we want to create.

It's a good idea to try producing short poems to 'punctuate' a writing day. Not only does this give us a break, it also freshens the mind, like cleansing the palate between the courses of a meal. It works particularly well when we feel blocked with our writing, as it takes the mind off the project we're engaged in without abandoning our writing altogether.

Generally, poetry produces its effects with fewer words than prose. In order to write poetry, we might have to think about structuring our writing within certain rules and conventions, using rhymes and rhythms. Even non-rhyming poetry without regular rhythm usually carries a sense of space and significance.

FIND BALANCE AND STABILITY

Restore balance and stability with this simple exercise.

Stand with your feet hip-width apart, shoulders relaxed, and chin tilted slightly upwards. Picture a thread that travels through the top of your head and down your spine. Imagine that this thread is being tugged gently and feel your spine gradually lengthening.

Turn your attention to the soles of your feet and feel the weight of your body as it's balanced equally through each leg. Bounce lightly, bending at the knees and notice how you are supported by the earth.

Draw your hands, palms together, and pull them in to your heart. Close your eyes and picture a yin yang symbol in the centre of your chest. Focus on this image for a few minutes, and breathe deeply.

The yin yang symbol is universally associated with balance; this combined with a physical exercise that focuses on posture and movement helps to promote a sense of stability and equilibrium.

The earth anchors me.

*I am in perfect balance
with nature.*

*I am exactly where
I need to be.*

*My mind, body and
soul are in harmony.*

RECIPE

SUMMER SORBET

This refreshing sorbet is best enjoyed in the garden on a hot summer's day. As you take a bite, close your eyes and reflect on the sounds around you: what can you hear? Perhaps it's birdsong or the gentle whirring of a mower.

SERVES 6

INGREDIENTS

- 150g (5^1/$_2$oz) peeled and deseeded cantaloupe melon
- 3 tbsp freshly squeezed lemon juice
- 60g (2^1/$_4$oz) raw agave nectar
- 18 fresh or frozen raspberries
- 3 tsp raw cacao nibs

EQUIPMENT

- power blender
- six 50-ml (2-fl oz) shot glasses

TIP
Add thyme or mint leaves after blending for a fresh, botanical flavour.

METHOD

1. Add the melon, lemon juice and agave nectar to your power blender and blend on full power until smooth.

2. Divide the mixture evenly between the 6 shot glasses. Add 3 raspberries to each glass, then ½ teaspoon cacao nibs sprinkled on top.

3. Place, uncovered, in the freezer for at least 6 hours or until frozen. The sorbets can be stored in the freezer for up to a month, although the fresher the better.

NATURE

SEEDBOMBS FOR SENSES

This mix has been designed to fill your nostrils with a heavenly sweet scent. See pages 112–113 for the base recipe and use the following seeds to create a feast for the senses.

PLANTS

- Cowslip *Primula veris*
- Feverfew *Tanacetum parthenium*
- Lady's Bedstraw *Gallium verum*
- Wild chamomile *Matricaria recutita*
- Wild marjoram *Origanum vulgare*
- Meadowsweet *Filipendula ulmaria*
- Sweet cicely *Myrrhis odorata*

SEEDBOMBS FOR BIRDS

The plants in this mixture attract insect larvae from which the birds will feed, as well as offering a rich seed source throughout the season. Birds help with seed dispersal and some seeds cannot germinate unless they have first passed through the digestive system of a bird.

The RSPB believes that a healthy bird population is indicative of a healthy planet and the human race depends on this.

Climate change, modern farming methods, road and rail networks, exploitation of our seas and expanding urban areas all pose an enormous threat to birds. We can try to increase the bird population by growing foodplants and creating healthy habitats for them to live and breed in.

PLANTS

· Wild mint *Mentha arvensis*
· Lemon balm *Melissa officinalis*
· Liquorice *Glycyrrhiza glabra*

COLOURFUL SEEDBOMBS

The plants in this mixture are perfect for adding a splash of colour to your garden and also as a cut flower in the home. These plants can be grown in sunny or shaded spots so you can have colour whatever the aspect your garden faces.

PLANTS FOR A SHADY/DAMP SPOT

· Self-heal *Prunella vulgaris*
· *Bergamot Monarda didyma*
· Borage *Boragio officinalis*

PLANTS FOR A SUNNY/DRY SPOT

· Common poppy *Papaver rhoeas*
· Arnica *Arnica montana*
· Purple coneflower *Echinacea purpurea*

WISHING LOVING-KINDNESS

There are 7.9 billion people on this planet and roughly half of them are in darkness at any one time. When you look up at the moon, there is a high chance that some of the other 3.9 billion people in darkness are also looking up at the moon at that moment. As we share that experience, how would it be to send out wishes of kindness to all those people – whoever they are, wherever they are and whatever they are going through in their life right now? You could try mentally saying, 'I wish for you all to feel safe, to feel at ease, to have good health, to feel contentment and peace'. As you send out these wishes, what is the response in your body? How do you feel?

If you are missing a friend or loved one, try looking up at the moon and asking them to do the same. You will feel instantly connected through your shared sight of the moon – the same moon, the same view.

PAINTING WITH THE BREATH

The breath has been woven through artistic practice throughout the ages, from the stencilled handprints of indigenous Australians – created by blowing delek (powdered white clay) from their mouths – to the controlled use of breath required in the practice of glass blowing. Developing mindfulness around how we use and cultivate our breath within artistic practice can help to bring us into the moment, with the potential of enhancing the way we work.

THE POWER OF BREATH

Breathing is an inherent and subconscious function of our nervous system, one that can be forgotten with ease. Yet it communicates with our mind and body. When we breathe deeply, particularly through the nose, we can create strong feelings of calm. When we unify our inhalation and exhalation with the movements of our body as we make our art, we consciously draw attention to our bodies. The concentration needed to maintain this brings us to mindfulness, while the synchronicity of it creates elegant and fluid movement. Holding the breath or slowing our exhalation relaxes our sympathetic nervous system, which is responsible for activating the fight or flight response.

BREATHING TO STILL THE MIND

Of course, concentrating on the breath can still the mind in a powerful way too. If we find our mind overactive, with an internal rhetoric drawing our attention away from our creative work, we can simply tune in to the soft rise and fall of our chest. As we focus on the coolness of the air as it passes into our nose and travels down our throat, expanding our lungs, we can bring a palpable rhythm to our practice and calm the busy mind. When we come to a tricky technical part of making, we may find we instinctively hold our breath. When we stop breathing we feel the passage of time more acutely, almost giving the illusion of slowing it. As we become more aware of our breath, we might choose to use it more deliberately in our mindful artistic practice.

We can take breathing for granted, as we do with so many other automated functions of the body. When we deliberately tune into our body and its usual patterns as part of our artistic practice, we can heighten our sensitivity to any changes in these rhythms. This enhances the mind–body connection, and with this we can foster a more mindful state in both our artistic creation and in daily life.

JULY

*Time to renew. Nature bathing,
eco-therapy and sky salutations
or simply being present in nature
rejuvenates our spirits.*

RED SKY AT NIGHT, SHEPHERDS' DELIGHT

Looking skywards in the evening at a beautiful pink sunset, we might recall the common expression echoed in many cultures: 'red sky at night, shepherds' delight'. When the white light of the Sun passes through the atmosphere it hits dust particles and water droplets. Blue light is scattered more easily than red, leaving the Sun itself to appear depleted of blue (and thus a yellowy colour) and the sky to look blue everywhere. At sunset, the Sun's rays glance through a thick column of atmosphere, and the blue gets scattered even more, changing the colour of the sky from yellow to pinky-red. A high concentration of dust particles in the atmosphere usually indicates high pressure and stable air – hence the shepherds' delight.

READING OUR INTERNAL WEATHER

Practising mindfulness offers us the opportunity to develop a finely tuned ability to read the internal weather of our being. What's your internal weather like right now? Mindfulness of our internal weather shows us that there is an ever-shifting 'feeling-tone' in our body which is only sometimes bubbling and excited, and other times dull, foggy, dark, overcast, clear, washed-out or brooding.

THE FOUR FOUNDATIONS

When the Buddha taught mindfulness, he spoke of what he called
'the four foundations': the body, our sensations, the mind and mind
objects. The body means things like posture, movement or the processes
of the body. Sensations are the things going on in the body, such as
temperature or pressure. The mind includes consciousness and the
constructs of the mind. And mind objects are the things that go on in
the mind, like thoughts, memories and ideas. It is possible to practise
mindfulness of the mind and mind objects, but it is very easy to be
carried away into thoughts and worries. Being mindful of the body and
its sensations is simpler. If we notice a tingling in the left palm, then
we just notice the tingling. If a storyline about the tingling does arise,
we can let it go and come back to the tingling sensation.

The Buddha taught that mindfulness in any of these four domains has
the potential to take us on the path to enlightenment.

A YOGA SEQUENCE
TO GROUND YOURSELF

DURATION: 10–15 minutes
YOGA STYLE: Classical Hatha
GOOD FOR: Grounding, calming, connecting with Earth energy

This sequence can help you connect with the energy of Mother Earth and ground excess energy. It is particularly useful if you work with others in a healing capacity and tend to pick up their energy. The postures balance the root chakra and are even more effective when practised outside, barefoot upon the ground.

Move consciously through the poses, holding them for 10–15 breaths (on each side when the pose is done on the left and right sides). Imagine that you have roots growing down into the Earth beneath you, linking you with the energy of nature. Visualize drawing this energy up through your roots and into your root chakra, located at the base of your spine.

Finish by lying on the ground outside for 2 minutes in Corpse Pose. If outdoor space isn't available to you, try to practise with some plant allies nearby.

1. GARLAND POSE

2. HERO POSE

3. HEAD-TO-KNEE POSE

4. ONE-LEGGED PIGEON POSE

5. LOW LUNGE

6. TREE POSE

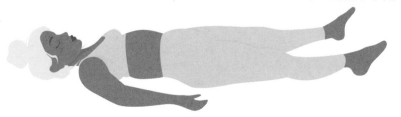

7. CORPSE POSE

CONNECT WITH A WATERFALL

Boost your vitality by connecting to the invigorating energy of the waterfall. Practise this visualization anytime and anywhere, whenever you need a pick-me-up.

Take a moment to relax, breathe deeply and calm your mind. Close your eyes and imagine you're standing beneath a glorious waterfall. You can feel the shimmering water flowing over you, hitting the top of your head and cascading over your shoulders. The tiny droplets are infused with magical energy, and they shine like diamonds.

As you breathe in, imagine the vibrant water passing through the top of your head, flooding your entire body with vitality. As you breathe out, picture the water flowing freely from the soles of your feet into a stream. Stretch each breath out for as long as possible and continue this loop of inhaling the diamond-bright energy and releasing it back to nature.

Do this for five minutes every morning to feel energized and ready for anything!

In folklore, the waterfall is a symbol of rejuvenation. It's associated with spiritual cleansing and connected to the crown chakra, located at the top of the head. The combination of the symbol and the breathing technique helps to cleanse and renew mind, body and spirit.

I am infused with energy.

*I am a dynamic soul and
I shine with vitality.*

Every day I am renewed.

THE WATERFALL

A BEDTIME MEDITATION FOR VITALITY

Before you, the water flows. You drink in the sight and sound of it rushing by, beating a path from the brow of the hill down to the forest floor. It cascades over the edge, tumbling down to create the most beautiful waterfall you have ever seen. It takes your breath away. You watch as it pools, a frothy white mass that loops and swirls down the mountainside. As you stand halfway up, you listen to the sounds, the whoosh and the whirr, the magical trickles that dance like musical notes above your head, and you long to be a part of the symphony. The water looks so pure and inviting. Like liquid crystal, it glistens in the afternoon sun. Everything it touches becomes more vibrant, as if lit from the inside.

You climb a little higher, feeling your way along each piece of rock until you are standing directly beneath this spectacle. A spray of fine droplets peppers your skin. Tiny pinpricks of moisture that make each pore tingle with joy.

You're infused with energy.

Your body feels almost fluid, as if you could change shape and navigate any landscape. Your mind too is alive and active. New ideas flood your vision, and you feel suddenly awake and ready to take on the world.

The waterfall continues to rush past, charged with a mission to reach the swell of the stream below. Nothing stands in its way. Nothing can stop it; such is the power and the potential of nature. You long to feel the same, to be charged with vigour. You reach out your hands, let the water hit your skin. It pelts each palm, wrapping around your fingers then slipping through them before you can grasp it. It taunts you, begs you to follow, to join in with this watery dance and let gravity take hold.

There is no decision to be made, no thought or preparation.

You are a dynamic soul and, in this moment, you can do anything. Stretching your arms to a point above your head, you dip forwards and plunge, joining forces with the waterfall. You are a darting, diving shadow amongst the sparkling stream. Svelte and lithe, you twist and turn, letting the water animate you. It's an easy passage and with each sweep of your arms, you feel more energized and able to let go. Full of verve and passion, you glide, not knowing or caring the direction, just delighting in your own vitality.

A surge of adrenalin powers through you, and you skim the surface during your downward descent. Your body ripples, pouring forwards until you become part of a much bigger body of water. Increasing in mass and drive, you are almost there, almost ready to hit the ground running. You take a gulp of air, drinking it down deep. The energy is exhilarating!

And then it happens, instant and invigorating; you reach the bottom, plunging beneath the glistening surface. You made it! You swam the waterfall, plummeted its dazzling depths and let it seep into your heart. The momentum of the fall has left you elated. For a moment you tread water and catch your breath. The cool stream gathers around you and you feel refreshed. Your spine bristles and your mind fizzes with energy. If you were despondent before, now you are renewed. The switch has been flicked and you are bubbling with anticipation.

You gaze up at the waterfall and find that you can no longer see where it starts or ends, how high it is or how it was created. It's as if the gushing rivulets are a cosmic gift from the universe. As if the heavens have opened and allowed the elixir of life to fall to earth. You realize then how blessed you are. Every day offers the chance of renewal, the opportunity for rebirth and to feel this invigoration. All you have to do is invite positive energy into your life.

Be open, be brave, and embrace your vibrance.

Slowly, you rise from the water, pulling yourself onto the damp mossy bank. You shake the droplets from your hair and marvel at your glistening skin. Upon your face is a wide smile. Your heart beats with passion, and you glow from head to toe.

Vitality is restored.

THE SCENT
OF THE GARDEN

Can you conjure up a scent memory of fresh rosemary leaves? Wet soil after a shower of rain? The first violet of spring? What are your scent associations with the garden? Smell ties us to place and experience as much as images and sounds; for some, smell might create even stronger associations and memories. Smell is the only fully developed sense at birth. Smell molecules go straight to the brain, accessing memory and stress centres directly. When we talk about scent, we often think of essential oils or other strong smells. But even subtle scents in the garden are part of what make us slow down and connect with the Earth.

Plants communicate through scent. The smell of freshly cut grass is a call for help. Flowers make scents that call to their specific pollinators, some sweet as vanilla (literally) and some distasteful (to us) as rotten flesh. The best-smelling plant might lead us to the most nutritious seeds, for instance.

Farmers historically used scent (and also taste) to determine the make-up and health of soil. We can still tell if soil contains lots of clay or organic material from its scent. The former smells dusty and damp, while the latter is sweeter and might smell mossy or like leaf litter. Soil that has too much ammonia or that smells rotten or swampy might indicate the need for aeration and added compost. We can add that to the list of mindful gardening tasks: besides plant smellers, we need soil smellers. Perhaps it's not a full-time job, but taking time to smell your soil, your plants and the compost in your garden will likely tell you something you don't have to search for online to understand.

THE SCENT OF MEMORIES

Scent is an important part of sensory gardens for people with visual impairment or other limitations. We can all enjoy sensory gardens, however, running our hands over the soft and pungent woolly thyme, inhaling the scent of chocolate cosmos and sniffing the pineapple mint. Scent is a way, therefore, that we can make our gardens more inclusive and compassionate. Include in your scent garden smells that take you back to a cherished garden memory, like your grandmother's roses, or lavender from that trip to Provence. What would you include in your sensory memory garden? All you need then is a meditation cushion or a bench, and you've created a healing garden of your own. If you live in a place without your own outside space, growing pots of herbs and create an aromatic, soothing environment. The scent garden can be a place to get to know yourself better, a place to invite trusted friends and share with them your stories, and invite them to share their own.

HEALING SEEDBOMBS

These mixtures have plants with healing properties for the mind, body and spirit. The plants will nourish and soothe, relax and enliven, as well as have culinary uses. Simply follow the recipe on pages 112–113 and include these botanical seeds in Step 2.

WELLBEING

· Lemon balm *Melissa officinalis*
· Borage *Boragio officinalis*
· Wild marjoram *Oreganum vulgare*
· Wild chamomile *Matricaria recutita*
· Liquorice *Glycyrrhiza glabra*

WAKE UP

· Wild mint *Mentha arvensis*
· Lemon balm *Melissa officinalis*
· Liquorice *Glycyrrhiza glabra*

SLEEP WELL

· Anise *Pimpinella anisum*
· Common thyme *Thymus vulgaris*
· Mugwort *Artemisia vulgaris*

BAREFOOT RUNNING

There is an increasing trend amongst runners to run barefoot, enjoying an even closer connection to the earth. Losing the shoes is like shedding a skin. You find yourself at the same time more vulnerable and more sensitive to all the earth has to offer. Running barefoot, you become aware of previously unsensed subtle changes in temperature and texture as you run over patches of sunlight on the trail, damp and dry soil or vegetation. You will know within a split second when you pass a spiky-leaved plant. As you expose yourself to the trail you feel so much more – every sensation is amplified; the connection to your surroundings has increased in its intensity. You are fully alive in the moment, all senses firing.

Running barefoot causes you to become more attentive to your own time and place. Barefoot runners claim to be happier and more injury-free without their shoes, but just bear in mind that it can take weeks and months to build up your foot strength and harden the skin on your feet necessary for faster or longer runs, and running on some terrain will always be a challenge with no shoes at all. All forms of running create a connection between us and the earth and remind us of our responsibilities to our world.

TREAD MINDFULLY ON THE EARTH

As you run, meditate on your footprint, think about your connection to the world and consider ways in which you can lighten your impact and reduce your carbon footprint. Reusing water bottles, choosing sustainable and fair-trade food and fabrics – as runners we can play our part. We owe it to ourselves and our futures to tread lightly and mindfully on the earth.

MAKING A POEM

There are so many varieties of poetry, and so many opinions as to what makes it 'good', that it is really almost beyond definition. However, it is generally agreed that one or both of the following characteristics relate to most poems:

· Word patterns, including rhythm and rhyme-schemes.
· The most apt, concise and original expression in words of emotions, experiences, sights and so on.

It can be fun to fit our words into a rhyming scheme, or follow a set kind of rhythm, but it's important with poetry to have confidence in your own voice, and write what feels right to you.

An interesting but simple way to start writing poetry is with the haiku. These little poems can help us think about the structure of any piece of writing. A haiku traditionally contains just 17 syllables within its three lines: 5 in the first line, 7 in the second and 5 in the third. The lines are not usually rhymed. Haikus tend to be lyric poems, expressing feelings or emotions, and often concern nature.

EXAMPLE HAIKUS

We hated the rain
But next day's puddles blessed us
With sky at our feet.

He left at sun-rise.
It was day-break for the world,
But heartbreak for me.

She smiled a welcome
From under her umbrella
And rainbowed his day.

*Try making haiku poems of your own.
Make sure you keep to the 17-syllable,
three-line form.*

UNLIMITED KINDNESS

There is a beautiful meditation practice, called 'mettā bhāvanā' in the original Pali, which can be translated as the 'cultivation of loving kindness', or 'development of unlimited friendliness'. This practice can have remarkable positive effects on you, your loved ones and the people you meet in daily life, particularly if practised regularly.

Begin by being aware of how you are, and try to create a warm glow of positive intention and love and appreciation within yourself. Think of it like starting a small fire to warm yourself up, and then try to create a brighter, larger fire to radiate outwards to other people. One method can be to begin by repeating phrases in your mind like, 'May I be well, may I be happy, may I be at peace'. This first stage can create an openness to the idea and intention.

The second stage is to imagine a good friend, or someone that brings a smile to your face. Try and see, hear or have a sense of them, as though you are with them. You can also repeat the phrases in relation to them – 'May you be well, may you be happy, may you be at peace' – and see how your imagination responds. Or, perhaps, imagine them enjoying something they love doing, like playing happily with their child or family, or doing an activity they love. Feel that sense of joy and fondness in contemplating them.

In the third stage, we start to spread that well-wishing intention outwards to people we may recognize but don't know so well, perhaps colleagues or teachers from school. Then radiate that goodwill out towards other people: children and families, people that live near you, and ultimately people throughout the globe. You can include the whole life cycle of humans from newborn babies, to toddlers, school children, teenagers, adults and elders. Wish them to be well, happy and be at peace.

There can be many beneficial results if you make a habit of this meditation. You may find yourself being more emotionally open and friendly towards people you don't know, or being able to sustain positive states of mind more easily and for longer. The regard for your own and other people's wellbeing and happiness is a precursor for many nurturing states of mind.

A WALK WITH
THE MOON AND STARS

A great time for a long walk is in the evening, when we can share the landscape of the countryside, or the urban scene of the city, with the setting of the sun and the coming of twilight; we observe the changing colours of the sky until, darkening, it begins to reveal the stars. Maybe there is also a moon.

As we walk, the heavens may trigger in us a troubling sense of our insignificance, our smallness in the face of the vast and ancient universe and the utter irrelevance of our short lives, or else they might inspire in us a calm sense of wonder. It all depends on how we think about it.

OUR PLACE ON THE PLANET

The sun itself is enough to make us feel small; at a million times the volume of the Earth, that fiery furnace – converting four million tons of its mass into light and heat every second, as it has done for over four billion years – is the star we know best. As it sets, its light is somewhat subdued and reddened by the atmosphere; we are able to contemplate what we owe to that great ball of nuclear energy, the essential powerhouse of the evolution of life on our planet. As it slips beneath the western horizon we may then turn to the east and observe the lilac shadow of our world rising up into the stratosphere, a prelude to the darkness that will reveal the stars.

Walking through twilight from daylight into darkness is a great time to be mindful of our place on the planet as it rolls towards the east through space, turning daily on its axis. For a moment we may imagine ourselves as viewed by a handful of astronauts from the moon – inhabitants of a blue and white bauble, a tiny world far from the sun, suspended in emptiness.

WE OWE ALL THIS TO THE STARS

The stars appear. If we are walking on a winter's evening and we live in the northern hemisphere, we will see the summer triangle of bright stars: Deneb in Cygnus the Swan, Vega in Lyra the Lyre and Altair in Aquila the Eagle. If the sky is really clear, without light pollution, we may be treated to a great view of the Milky Way running down to the southern horizon, a haze of millions of stars, all of them suns – many much bigger than our own local sun. And if we were to stop and contemplate their distances, they would undoubtedly challenge our powers of thinking.

As we walk in the dark, perhaps along a familiar path, eschewing the use of a torch, we are aware of the trees overhead, silhouettes of branches through which the stars twinkle; an owl hoots from woodland; our nostrils are assailed by the smell of new-mown hay; we breathe in and out mindfully, tasting the night air. We owe all this to the stars. Without them we would not be here.

AUGUST

*Time to flow. Blue mindfulness
reconnects us to a natural
element to cherish and
revere in all its forms.*

TUNING IN TO THE TIDES

The tides are the lungs of the ocean, rising and falling. An in-breath – the moon moves closer to the earth and pulls at the body of water, stretching its skin. An out-breath as the moon moves away – the skin of the ocean relaxes back and the tide subsides.

The tide is a timepiece. The word 'tide' comes from the old English and German words for 'time' (tid and Zeit). Tidal flow is an affordance of mindfulness. It locks us into rhythms. The word 'rhythm' comes from the ancient Greek root, meaning 'to flow' – and so we come back to water and the sea in all its restless states.

In Cornwall, the smell of coconut and pineapple emanates from gorse blossom in spring and early summer, while once-rare choughs (birds that are the Cornish emblem) hover above the cliff sides. Adders might cross your path, looking for a place to sun themselves as you race down the cliff, board in tow, a swell running. Above, a kestrel eyes its prey.

With a grinding swell and a rising tide, the sea will race to deposit its entire weight on the beach in powerful pulses. This is particularly impressive during spring tides, where the sun and moon align and increase the gravitational pull on the ocean. The energy is tangible.

THE MAGIC OF GRAVITATIONAL PULL

The combined effect of the moon and sun varies throughout the month. When moon and sun are in concert (at full moon and new moon) this produces the largest tidal ranges (spring tides). At so-called 'first quarter' and 'last quarter' the moon and sun work against each other, resulting in smaller tidal ranges (neap tides).

It is a remarkable phenomenon, two gravitational forces pulling at the elastic body of the world's oceans as they either join together or stand opposed. If it were strong enough, the Moon's gravitational pull would strip the Earth of its waters and scatter them into space. But, of course, the tides are by no means weak. They are a majestic force, and arguably the most reliable source of energy available.

Complementing this tidal flux are weather changes. Water evaporates from the seas and returns as rain. Big tides often come with dramatic weather shifts. The sea seems to suck in the sky's temper. A glowering sky, threatening rain or a thunderstorm, is absorbed into the sea and filters down.

Sitting there, in the swell, with lightning about to be thrown down, brings home how small the human figure is against the immensity of the ocean. These are times when surfing really reminds us how the body is transient, just a punctuation mark in the long narrative aeons of Earth.

MINDFUL RUNNING

Mindful running offers an adventure to those who choose to pursue it, a feeling that will feed into all aspects of our lives and nourish the darkest corners of our worlds. Running gives us the opportunity to stay connected with the world and with ourselves. A mindful perspective can bring a new depth to your running, a greater awareness of where it can take you and how much you can achieve. The freedom that running gives us is the ideal opportunity to practise mindful techniques, whether on a day-long cross-country expedition or a quick circuit around the block. Lacing up and heading out mindfully can be a powerful force for wellbeing – more dynamic than just mindfulness, and more rewarding than just running. You may not find flow on every run but in the long term you will certainly reap the rewards.

FINDING CLARITY

The many physiological benefits of running include improving our cardiovascular health, strengthening our bones and lowering cholesterol. Psychologically, running can reduce stress, improve our self-esteem and result in feelings of positivity. Introducing mindfulness into your running routine will bring further advantages as you set your mind free and focus on the moment, simply putting one foot in front of the other and acknowledging your surroundings as they pass by, finding harmony and serenity in your actions.

LIVING IN THE MOMENT

Running is complementary to mindfulness; many runners will be practising mindfulness to some degree through their actions without any conscious attempt to do so. Through the repetitive footfalls and breathing we find it relatively easy to move to a place where body and mind move as one. Absorbed in the action of running, our minds are stilled; we are able to dwell in the present, enjoying the sensations of the body and thus being released from our daily anxieties. This regular release spills over into the rest of the day and further into our lives; when we are in possession of a calmer mind and greater clarity, we can deal better and more intuitively with our day-to-day challenges.

THE MAGIC OF PHOTOSYNTHESIS

Inside all the beautiful green leaves of the plant kingdom, magic occurs. Some call it science, but really it is both. Photons of light bounce off chlorophyll molecules, setting off a chain of events that produces plant energy in the form of glucose, and the by-product of oxygen. Because of this 'technology' created by plants 450 million years ago, we are alive today. We grow photosynthesis factories in our gardens. Whether you regard the process as purely scientific or a miracle, or both, you tuck little seeds into soil as an invocation of photosynthesis. A garden or a farm is a request of the universe to please transform sunlight, carbon dioxide and water into energy that we can use to dance and dream and love. Most of the time, this request is honoured, and we get both fresh air and salad in the process. Miraculous!

Plants photosynthesize without thinking about it. They don't have to try to make sugar, they just do. Perhaps we can learn from them in this – be grateful for the natural processes our bodies carry out without conscious effort, and express our gifts just as 'something we do'. Sometimes our gifts feel easy to execute, and we feel nourished by them. At other times, they feel more like a chore, or expressing our gifts pushes against self-doubt or fear. We can remember the plants photosynthesizing for the good of all, and settle into our own gifts without fear.

EXPRESSING OUR LIGHT

Photosynthesis is respiration in reverse. Respiration is essentially breathing, and it means to re-spirit, to re-breathe. We breathe, and we are filled with spirit again and again. Whether we breathe mindfully as we sit still as a rooted plant, or we re-spirit as we garden in a moving meditation, we reflect the natural processes of energy production and transformation of light. In spiritual teachings across cultures, we are also made of light, the bright light that glows within. Expressing our gifts – in a balanced dance of give and take – is a way we share this light with the world. 'Synthesis' means to put together, so we perform our own version of photosynthesis – putting together light – when we take the experiences we have had, our natural gifts and the skills we have developed, synthesize them and share them with the world.

AWAKENING THE WORDS

Writing is a way of speaking our thoughts to the world, whether or not we want to share with others what we've written. It is also a kind of self-care, allowing us to take the time to listen to our own minds and to express our inner thoughts, concepts and feelings. To do this successfully, we need a wide-awake awareness of ourselves, our needs and the workings of our minds. Through writing mindfully, we get to know ourselves better, shape ideas and harvest the produce of our imaginations.

Mindfulness helps us to harness our creativity, providing easy focus and control. We begin as children, listening to stories, and generating more in our imaginations. Then a kind teacher shows us how to write. After that, there should be no stopping us; the world is full of bright inspiration, and we have the potentiality to ignite our own magic from this collective fire. But many of us lack the confidence to express ourselves in words. We doubt our right to speak, and fear the judgement of others. Any other task can seem to have priority over the desire to write. Such worries are simple distractions, but they disrupt our concentration and impede our vision. With mindfulness, we can see these distractions for what they are, and learn the present-moment awareness which is vital to our writing.

MINDFUL MOMENTS IN NATURE

Building time in nature into our week, or better yet into our day's routine, means we are actively choosing how we experience the world around us. Not rushing through it, nor simply stopping to smell the roses, but going deeper still. Looking past the obvious beauty of the roses and taking in all aspects of nature shows us that beauty can also exist in decay, in the mundane – a fallen leaf, a dying flower, a broken cobweb – and in the ignored aspects of our life. When your eyes are opened to seeing and experiencing the subtle intricacies of beauty in nature around you, you naturally slow into a more mindful process of being in the world.

THE HEALING POWER OF WATER

Use the power of water to boost healing, by incorporating these top tips into your schedule. Infuse body and soul with healing energy throughout the day by sipping water. This will keep you hydrated and also help you to remain focussed in challenging situations. Imagine that each mouthful is imbued with positive energy, which surges through you as you drink.

If you need an extra boost of vitality, run the cold tap and place your wrists underneath the flow of water for at least a minute. As you do this, picture a stream of white light travelling up each arm and around your entire body. Breathe deeply and relax.

Alternatively fill the sink with cold water and submerge your hands. Close your eyes and imagine you are dipping your hands into the sea.

Running cold water on your wrists lowers the body's core temperature and heart rate and helps to reduce levels of cortisol, the stress hormone. This coupled with a relaxing visualization will make you feel instantly calmer.

All is good, all is calm.

I surrender to the ebb and flow.

I release pain, I let it go.

Healing energy washes over me.

MINDFUL WRITING

To write mindfully is to imagine yourself back in the time of quill and paper or retro typewriter, and to flout expediency in exchange for a slowed and conscious approach to our use of words. Compose a sentence. Stop and take a breath. Look at the sentence and consider what it actually says. Does it communicate clearly and accurately what you wanted to say? Consider the readability of the text. Change it if you need to before moving on with the next sentence or paragraph. Take the rush out of the writing. Acknowledge that word count does not indicate progress. The measure of success might instead be the accuracy of communication and the shape and form of prose as gracefully and intentionally crafted as a sculpture made from a single stone. The measure of success might also be the experience of writing as something pleasurable. Revel in the variety and possibly of words and the potential they give for communication and for understanding.

THE AESTHETIC OF WRITING

There is an aesthetic quality to writing. We need not always be on our computer. You might perhaps change to pencil and paper for your draft. Feel the grip of your fingers around your pencil. Hear the scratch of the graphite on paper and feel the subtle friction of it against the surface. Perhaps write with a calligraphy pen, a process which requires a certain awareness and embodied presence, engaging visually with the ink and using it with a sense of control, watching it as it dwindles, observing its change in flow and re-inking before it runs dry. Even the clatter of striking your computer keys can produce a kind of musical rhythm which can bring with it a feeling of delight.

WRITING WITH INTENTION

While mindful awareness in writing can be exemplified by the slow and considered use of language and the embodied physical experience of writing, there is also a place for the thundering, surrendering outpouring of free writing. There is nothing like taking the handbrake off and writing fast and free, letting your words flow without judgement or consideration or care for correct spelling or grammar, allowing for whatever is arising in your mind to spill onto the page without hesitation. This sort of writing can purge writers' block, energize us and help us find an elusive phrase or expression trapped inside. Free writing is authentic writing, which occupies the mind so well we simply cannot be diverted. After such a deluge you may find the mind stilled once again, ready to softly engage with slow and considered writing once more, until staleness ensues and you are once again ready to run.

Mindful writing is writing with intention. It is being present in the act of writing, embodying the physical experience and observing the mental experience. When we write mindfully, we use the practice of writing as the focus for our meditation, during which we witness ourselves in the creative act. What beauty such an experience of writing might bring to the author.

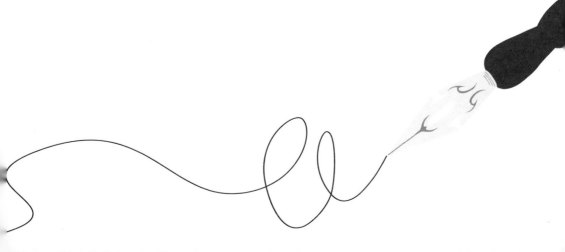

LEMON BALM
Melissa officinalis

Lemon balm is a commonly grown plant used as a household remedy; it has traditionally been made into a tonic to lift the spirits. The Latin name for lemon balm, 'Melissa', is Greek for honey bee; the bees love to feed from the nectar-rich flowers, which appear throughout the summer. The seeds are best harvested in August and this is when cuttings can be taken too.

STEMS Wiry, square-branched upright stems.

LEAVES The green lemon-scented broad leaves are serrated and grow opposite each other up the stem.

FLOWERS The flowers are nectar-full hermaphrodite, 1.3cm (½in) long, white tubular in shape with two lips.

SEEDS 1mm (¹/₂₅in) long, smooth, black and oval-shaped.

LAUNCH SEEDBOMBS April and September.

GERMINATION TIME 1–3 weeks.

HARVESTING SEEDS The seed heads are ripe for harvest August–October.

PLANT CARE Regular trimming will promote fresh young leaf growth and prevent vigorous spreading. To keep foliage flavoursome, cut back some of the flowering stems but leave a few for the bees to enjoy. Divide in spring or autumn and take cuttings in July/August. It will self-sow readily from seed and can be propagated by taking stem cuttings, which will root easily if placed in a jar of water. Can be invasive as it grows quickly and spreads easily. A way of tackling this in small cultivated beds is to grow it in a pot and sink the pot into the ground. Lemon balm requires regular watering but does not require any feeding.

CULINARY AND MEDICINAL USES The leaves are the main edible parts used for their lemon aroma and flavour; they can be eaten raw or cooked. Lemon balm can be used to flavour soups, salads, sauces, poultry stuffings and vegetables, beverages like tea and iced and alcoholic drinks. Lemon balm has been long used because of its antibacterial and antiviral properties to help treat digestive problems, coughs, colds and flu, menstrual cramps and toothache, for dressing wounds and, according to studies, to calm the nerves and soothe tension. In the Middles Ages it was used as a cure-all plant to treat skin eruptions and cricked necks and to relieve morning sickness.

OTHER USES Even after harvesting, the leaves and flowers have a long-lasting aroma and can be used as a potpourri. The crushed leaves rubbed on the skin can be used as a mosquito repellent.

THE PERSEID METEOR SHOWER

The Perseus constellation is best known for its annual Perseid meteor shower, one of the most prominent meteor showers in the sky, visible from mid-July each year to everyone living north of 17°S. The peak activity is usually in mid-August.

If you have ever tried watching for a meteor (shooting star) you will know it's a frustrating business. Someone says 'Look, there!' and by the time you've turned, it's gone! Meteors provide a fleeting moment of glory as a small piece of space rock burns up in our atmosphere. In contrast to the seemingly unchanging night sky, they remind us of the constant dance of the Universe and the changing nature of things. Nothing is fixed: some things change quickly (like a meteor) and some things change too slowly for us to perceive (the movement of stars and galaxies), but you can be sure that underneath it all, everything is on the move.

TOUCHING A CITY'S HISTORY

The city is a trove of places that invite us to use our sense of touch as well as our eyes and ears. Botanic gardens and public parks are the obvious candidates. But fountains, sculptures and old brickwork can also offer us sensory pleasure. Running one's hand through a lively jet of water as it sparkles in the sunlight is a playful, childlike pleasure – and, moreover, this action of reaching out is instinctive to us to perform, bringing a simple enjoyment that can also ground us.

Placing a hand on a revered monument can make us more mindful of what it represents. But it can also remind us of the countless people who have stood in the same spot and taken spiritual solace from it, or of crucial moments that shaped a city's history. Touch is a way to feel this knowledge.

The historical places around our cities give us many opportunities to engage with ideas and people in a more contemplative way than if we had read the information in a book. Using our hands to experience them can connect us to people who may have lived before us, leading to a deeper understanding of that city's psychological identity.

WE SHARE THE WORLD

With birds we have a window into the natural world. Birdwatching, with or without binoculars, can be one of the most accessible and enjoyable ways to meditate on the rich global ecosystem we inhabit. In this vast and ancient universe, the evolution of life on Earth, with all its biodiversity, is a miracle – and we, astonishingly, are part of it. We just need to give the mind a rest, to watch and listen.

There are almost 10,000 avian species, from the tiny bee hummingbird and pygmy kingfisher to the giant condor and wide-winged albatross. They float through our skies, dive deep in our oceans, lurk in the shadowy undergrowth of forests and stalk the open plains. They are everywhere. Getting to recognize and know them can be a source of pure delight. It can also give us a way to deepen our sense of conscious living, to become more aware of who we are and how we came to be here, and to be more mindful of our role as human beings sharing in the intricate web of life of this glorious but fragile world.

In birdwatching, we learn patience and how to be still – gentle skills much needed in the noisy, busy and anxiety-ridden modern life that many people are forced to endure. The activity of birdwatching can itself be a form of mindfulness, calming both heart and mind.

We may wonder sometimes what the natural world will be like for future generations. The human destruction of habitats through agribusiness and urbanization, the pollution of oceans with plastics and poisons, and the careless use of pesticides are all pushing some species over the edge into extinction.

We have a duty to take responsibility for the health of the natural world. When we do not acknowledge that responsibility, it is because we have not become truly mindful of the fact that we too are part of nature.

CONNECTING TO THE OUTSIDE WORLD

Being part of our environment, rather than sitting separate to the world, is an aspect of mindfulness that allows us to feel and think in a deeper manner. It demands of us a compassion that can be missing with too much internal conversation or intense focus on our work. When we look around and notice other people, wildlife or nature – even simply let the sun settle on our face for a moment – we move outside ourselves and become more deeply connected with the world around us. Living in society with others means we become better human beings when we show connection and compassion, rather than only looking inwards at our own work, and only breathing or thinking or feeling our own emotions. Rushing towards finished projects, deadlines and expectations, or even simply appointments and events, means we are rarely centred or connected to the moment, or to the people we're surrounded by, but rather are caught up in a whirlwind that we have no control over.

Learning to stop and take a break, will hopefully help you to remember during a busy work day, or with the noise of children around you, to step back, even just for one moment, and simply do nothing but soak up the sunshine or feel the breeze upon your face. Often we are so caught up in our work that the very simple task of sipping water is forgotten,

Setting time aside during the day to put down our tools, leave our work behind and replenish our bodies is vital to a healthy way of living, and a peaceful outlook on life. While it may seem counter to popular practice, it will allow you to notice how deeply you needed the space, time and quiet. A break can be as simple as stepping outside into the garden, or standing up straight and looking at the sky, but this moment of stopping work allows your body the chance to stretch and re-energize itself, your eyes the opportunity to focus on something else for a moment, and your brain the space to stop the whirling thoughts.

AUTUMN

SEPTEMBER

OCTOBER

NOVEMBER

AUTUMN PLAYLIST

· *Autumn Sweater* – Yo La Tengo

· *California Dreamin'* – The Mama & The Papas

· *Harvest Moon* – Neil Young

· *Autumn Town Leaves* – Iron & Wine

· *My Cosmic Autumn Rebellion* – The Flaming Lips

· *I Am The Black Gold Of The Sun* – Nuyorican Soul

· *Meet Me At The Equinox* – Death Cab For Cutie

*I respect nature's rhythms
and my own.*

Leaves fall and rise, as do I.

Winds breathe in change, as will I.

SEPTEMBER

Time to harvest. Grow what we eat and eat what we grow. Gardening is a simple way to connect to the earth and nature's cycles of life.

THE MESSAGE OF THE GARDEN

Certainly, it just feels good to be around plants. When you grow them yourself, you cultivate unique relationships directly with plants.

Keeping food local and fresh is a powerful act of presence and responsibility. Growing your own food is one of the best things you can do for yourself and for the planet. Grow a little extra and you spread the nourishment to others. Whether you keep a little pot of herbs in the kitchen or you grow a farm's worth, bringing mindfulness to your garden can extend the important work of gardening into the realm of spiritual practice and emotional health.

There is so much more to a garden than the plants themselves. A garden is nutrients and soil, bees and nematodes, water and light. When we begin to explore all the different parts of a garden, including ourselves, we see how vast and complex the garden truly is. We begin to see ourselves as a part of a greater whole. We see how our actions affect other parts of that whole, and how they in turn affect us. In this way, the garden is a tool for compassion and deeper understanding. It's a wisdom we come to by doing, though reading about the garden can guide us to a different sort of knowing, too.

The message of the garden is the same everywhere. The plants, and the beings that support them, ask nothing of you but respect and care. They do not see your struggles and they do not judge. They invite you to be in relationship with them, separate but connected. Gardens reflect to us our essential nature, alive, seeking the light, hopeful for the future but unattached. Perhaps these thoughts do the same, inviting you to breathe, stretch and come back to your essential self.

MOVEMENT

HEAD-TO-KNEE POSE

Janu Sirsasana

DURATION: 5 minutes
YOGA STYLE: Vinyasa yoga
GOOD FOR: Stress relief, calming

Sit with your legs extended. Tilt your pelvis back so you are seated on the front of your sitting bones. Bend your left knee and bring your left sole to your inner right thigh. Firm the core and right thigh, extend through your heel and flex your feet. Inhale, drop your shoulders and reach your arms up. Exhale and fold forwards over your right leg, clasping your shin, ankle or foot. Keep the spine and extended leg straight. Inhale to return to the starting position and repeat on the other side.

MODIFICATIONS

Sit on a folded blanket and use a strap or belt hooked over the foot of the extended leg to maintain a straight spine.

VARIATION: ROUNDED SPINE (YIN YOGA)

Keep the knee softly bent, round the spine and rest the head on a folded blanket or block placed on the thigh.

HEAD-TO-KNEE POSE

GRATITUDE FOR TOOLS

As mindful makers, gratitude and respect for our tools and equipment is something that should be cultivated. We makers have tools and materials in our hands almost every day; some can last us a lifetime, while others might only be used a handful of times. Our modern throwaway society seems intent on creating things that aren't designed to last longer than a short season of use, forcing us to purchase more, but it doesn't have to be this way. If we look closely at how we use and care for our tools, we may well find we can make them last longer. Not only does this mean we are caring for our individual tools, and the wider environment, but it also gives us a more thoughtful approach to other possessions in our life and makes us grateful for what can be achieved with those tools.

A SENSE OF COMMUNITY

In a community of gardeners, each of us has something to bring to the group. Our unique backgrounds, our families, where we are in life and what we are passionate about – all are like ingredients for stone soup. In the story of Stone Soup, a clever fellow asks the members of a community to each contribute to his soup, which so far consists only of water and a stone. Each person brings one item – a carrot, a potato, some salt. In the end everyone gets a bowl of soup and new friends.

Sometimes gardeners can be more like the stone, sitting alone, doing our own thing. But even for those of us who are natural introverts, connecting with other like-minded gardeners strengthens our gardens and our own lives.

A COMMUNITY IS BORN

In Buddhism, a community is called a sangha. The spiritual sangha is based on the qualities of awareness, acceptance, understanding, harmony and love. An ideal gardening community would also include these qualities. As gardeners, we come from many different backgrounds, spiritual paths and gardening approaches, but we can all come together in a love of green and growing things. Community members can share the joy and pride of growing food or flowers. We can get excited about new techniques and resources. We can support each other when things don't go well. When they want to celebrate, we can be there with a healthy dish to cheer them on. Love of the Earth and of each other are the foundations of our connection. Plants are powerful community builders, as we all rely on plants each day.

ACROSTICS

A fun way to play with words while engaging your creativity is to write acrostics. An acrostic is a type of verse where the initial letters of each line can be read together to make a word, which is in effect the title of the verse. Using someone's name as the title for an acrostic is quite popular; this could be used in a greetings card as an original and affectionate or humourous tribute to a friend. Whatever word or name is chosen as a title, it is intended to be in some way commented on or defined by the verse. Each line will generally not be very long, as acrostics tend to be concise.

CELLPHONE

Call me any time
Everywhere I go
Loud and clear, it will sound,
Linking me with the world.
Perhaps it's too much;
Have I become over-reliant?
Other belongings mean nothing;
Need of my phone is paramount,
Every day, every hour, every moment.

EXPAND YOUR ENERGY

Close your eyes and imagine your spirit slipping out of a hole at the top of your head. Your ethereal body expands, and you can feel your energy growing in every direction. Look around the space and see yourself from above, then expand further. Imagine your spirit body seeping through the walls that enclose you. Imagine it stretching in every direction. You can see for miles above and below and still you continue to grow, reaching up towards the sky and above the clouds. See the vastness of the universe and know that you are a part of this. You can go anywhere and be anything. There are no limits.

Say 'There are no limits' three times with feeling, then continue on with your day with a renewed sense of freedom.

The affirmation coupled with the mini visualization instantly takes you out of yourself and brings you into the current moment, while providing a vision of cosmic potential.

This is my moment.

I relish the dance of life.

*I am free to be what
I want to be.*

*Ready for adventure,
ready for anything!*

COME RAIN OR SHINE

More important when dealing with the elements is our state of mind. How we perceive the weather is only partly dictated by the conditions but is strongly influenced by how we are feeling, and we can change this by using mindful techniques. Imagine yourself heading out on a run; it's a beautiful sunny day with a cooling breeze. The world feels alive and bright, the greenery is radiant, the hills are sharp against the horizon, the sunlight is glinting playfully off the surface of the water and the refreshing wind is whispering in the long grass. As you run you start to get tired; before you know it you are focusing on the heat, it feels overpowering, the wind is blowing against you and the glare of the sun off the surface of the water is blinding. Nothing has changed in the weather; your unhelpful thoughts are taking over and a negative perception of the elements is developing. By employing a little mindfulness we can change our frame of mind and our mental approach to facing the elements. We can return that unremitting glare and searing heat back to bright sunlight and brilliant views.

It seems we rarely allow ourselves to accept the weather, to enjoy just being present in what the world has given us today. We fight and rail against the conditions. We can be so negative that sometimes we can't even enjoy the present for fear of what may be around the corner. Some people are never happy – too icy, too hot, too wet, too windy and even when the weather appears to be perfect, 'Well I don't suppose it will last'. We delight in our elemental battles.

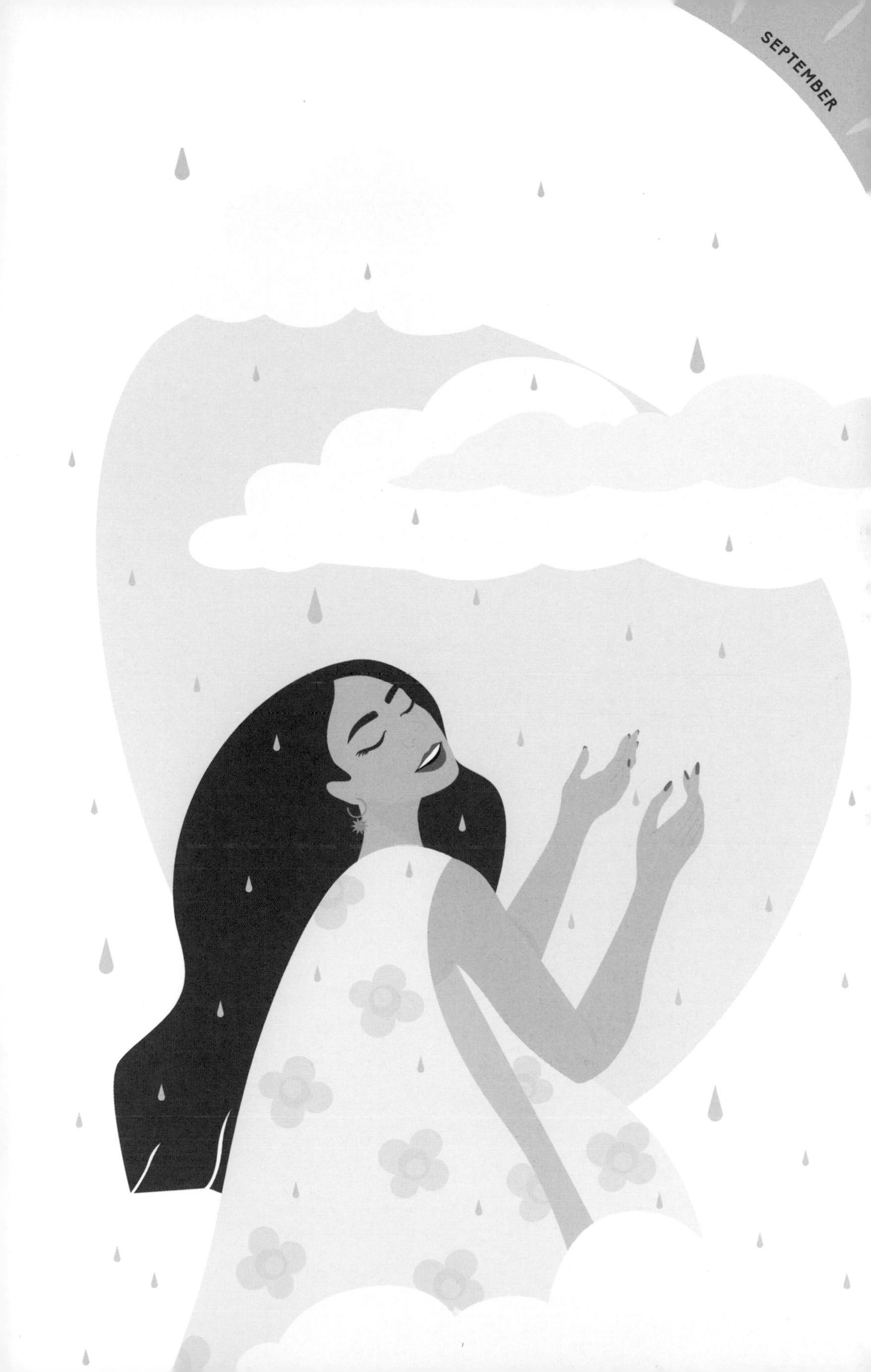

SUNFLOWER
Helianthus annuus

Native to the Americas, sunflowers were originally cultivated by Native Americans for their nutritious seeds. A member of the Asteraceae family along with all other daisy flowers, this annual plant is well loved for its sunshine-like flowers. October is the ideal time to harvest the seeds.

STEMS Rough, hairy woody.

LEAVES Broad, coarsely toothed, rough and growing alternately up the stem, getting smaller the higher up they grow. The leaves at the base of the plant are arranged opposite. The leaves have serrated edges, are 10–30cm (4–12in) long and range from triangular to heart-shaped, they have hairs on the upper and underside.

FLOWERS The flower heads consist of numerous small individual five-petaled florets. The outer flowers resemble petals and are called ray flowers. Sunflowers are Hermaphrodite. The flowers in the centre of the head are called disk flowers and are arranged in a spiral, they mature into seeds.

SEEDS Ripen from September–October.

LAUNCH SEEDBOMBS Early spring in pots and mid-spring in situ.

GERMINATION TIME 14 days

HARVESTING SEEDS The seeds are ripe when the flower heads start to dry and turn to face the ground. Cut off flower heads keeping 20cm (7¾in) of the stem attached and hang them upside down inside a pillow case. After a few days you can rub the seeds out gently with your hand or a brush, or if you have two seed heads try rubbing them together.

PLANT CARE Grow in full sun, in fertile, moist but well-drained soil, pH 5.7–8.5. Sunflowers are happy in dry, poor to average soil and need little water or fertilizer.

PESTS AND DISEASES Banded sunflower moth, cutworm, slugs, snails, downy mildew, powdery mildew, rust.

CULINARY AND MEDICINAL USES The seeds have a delicious nut-like flavour and are rich in fats so can be made into oil or butter or ground up and used in baking. The sprouted seeds can be eaten raw. A tea made from the leaves is thought to be useful as an astringent, diuretic or expectorant.

WHAT CYCLING IS REALLY ABOUT

Cycling is about freedom. The bike provides a means of escape from the confines of home, work, the phone and the inbox – a chance to, temporarily, drop off the radar and disappear. It is also about reconnecting with and being aware of feelings, physical sensations and the world around us. It is about confronting and overcoming challenges, fears and limits. It is about self-reliance and independence, and also the company of others, and encounters with strangers. It is about recapturing a sense of childlike wonder, and turning back the clock to simpler, more innocent days. It is about being in nature, on her level and terms, and directly sensing the long, slow roll of the seasons. It is about a new appreciation of the laws of physics, and finding ways to bend them, even while they remain unbreakable. It is, above all, about awareness. The modern world sometimes makes this difficult, with its constant distractions, pressures, demands and expectations. The bike gives us so many other, different things to focus on. How the legs are feeling, the texture of the road, changes in temperature, an approaching vehicle, a wild creature briefly glimpsed, a new sound from the transmission, a tight bend on a steep descent – all bring us back to the immediate moment. And when we're in that present, mindful state, all else fades into the background. If, at this moment, the bike is still moving forwards, you are climbing the hill you thought was impossible. From this realization comes resilience.

BRINGING QUIET TO A NOISY WORLD

To learn, through practice, how creativity and being a mindful maker can slow your mind, shows us ways to live in quietness and find contentment in the quiet, mundane moments of our life. When you listen to your own heartbeat, and understand your breath, you can take this practice into the world and utilize it to bring slow mindfulness into everyday life. Until you've tried this yourself, it might seem strange or too hard to do, but through regularly seeking the quiet in each day, you'll learn that you can take that quiet into the busyness of the world. Teaching yourself to tune into the stillness around you, perhaps watching a raindrop fall from a leaf, you'll find that you will continue to actively seek stillness and quiet when faced with a regular day of noisy, stressful moments. Using the calmness that making can give you, and understanding that it is possible, you will find a new way of being.

When you focus your mind on one noise or thing, your heart tunes into the sound of your creative work and you can slow time to just that moment.

THE QUIET IN THE MAKING

One of the joys of being a maker is finding moments of quiet space to create our work. In this ever-busy world we live in, sometimes stepping away from the noise can help us to find a deeper sense of meaning in our work. While it is true that not every aspect of our creative lives needs to be imbued with hushed tones, it is beneficial for our minds and our work when we actively seek the internal quiet. The chatter of a knitting circle or a companion in your studio or at your kitchen table is always a welcome addition to the pleasure of sitting and creating something. But if you are always in company, with noise around you, it makes it harder to find the space needed to contemplate the depth of your creative work. Stepping outside group activities and sitting by yourself in the quiet of the day is an important part of any maker's process. It might seem hard to replace the enjoyment of creating alongside someone else with the endless silence of working alone, but once you have experienced you internal quiet it makes those moments seem more profoundly special, and something to seek out.

INSPIRATION FROM WITHIN

Conversations with our inner self during moments of creativity give us a deeper insight into who we are, and how we fit into the human world. Being a maker gives us the opportunity to delve into aspects of ourselves that are often overlooked in the everyday noise of life. It gives us a chance to tap into our innate creativity and ignore the external critics while we immerse ourselves in the joy of making. Of course, not every craft has the opportunity every day for quiet self-reflection, but unless we try to bring some moments of quiet into the act of making, we may end up spending too long looking outside for inspiration, rather than finding it internally.

Noticing which techniques during your practice best fit the quiet, mindful flow of internal conversation means you can schedule those practices during times when no one else is around. The quietest times in your day can coincide with the more mindful aspects of your practice. Working within the creative zone allows for things to flow without being over-analysed or self-judged. This can often result in sheer beauty in the finished piece – and at the very least you'll have had a peaceful session at your work table.

OCTOBER

*Time to rediscover. Tune into
all your senses and discover
the world anew.*

A FOREST WALK

Trees were growing on the planet, pumping moisture into the atmosphere, breathing out oxygen, stirred by the wind in early dawns, long before we were here to see them. They saw the dinosaurs come and go, witnessed the appearance of the first flowering plants, and laid down the great coal deposits that fuelled the Industrial Revolution. Individually, they can live for many hundreds of years. Walk amongst trees and you share the air and the light with some of the oldest living beings on Earth.

A THREE-DIMENSIONAL EXPERIENCE

Some of the pleasure of walking in a forest is the way it demands that you look about you in every direction, peering up, down, around and deep into its depths – not because it is scary, but because it is a three-dimensional experience. The canopy above your head is as interesting as the ground beneath your feet; the undergrowth and ferns close by the path are as eye-catching as the trunks of the trees. Stands of straight timber, like the pillars of a great cathedral, reveal intriguing caverns of space, dark and mysterious. The walker can't help looking between and beyond the brush, the branches and the trunks, probing the half-light and the shadows.

You instinctively walk slowly through a wood or forest, as though venturing on to hallowed ground. There is so much to take in, the senses alerted from every direction – the smell of loam and rotting leaves, the noisy clatter of a wood pigeon flying off, the crackle of broken twigs as some startled creature, glimpsed for a moment in the dappled light, disappears into the dense undergrowth.

Find a place to stop. Get intimate. Feel the texture of a tree trunk, the smooth flanks of a beech or the rough, spongy and punchable bark of a redwood. Breathe deeply and inhale the smell of the humus on the forest floor. If possible, find a place to sit, a log perhaps, or if you are lucky and you are walking the forest path in a park, there may be a bench. This would be a good spot to do a mindful breathing exercise.

Take time. Recognize any distracting or troubling thoughts you may have; acknowledge them and let them go. Focus on the air as you inhale slowly, opening your lungs then exhaling without effort. Become aware of yourself as a breathing body sitting amongst trees.

STANDING CRESCENT POSE
Indudalasana

DURATION: 2–3 minutes
YOGA STYLE: Modern yoga
GOOD FOR: Increasing concentration, energizing the body

Begin in Mountain Pose, feet together or slightly apart. Rotate your palms to face front. Inhale and sweep your arms out to the side and upwards so that the palms connect above your head. Keep your shoulders down away from your ears, especially when your hands touch at the top. Stretch your hands towards the sky and root down through your feet. Exhale and bend to the right, keeping the left shoulder stacked on top of the right. Inhale to return to centre. Repeat on the left. To exit, exhale and float your arms back down.

MODIFICATIONS

Keep your feet hip-width and your hands
shoulder-width apart.

VARIATION: ONE LEGGED (INTERMEDIATE)

When bending to the right, lift the right leg sideways
towards the right arm. Exhale to release the leg back
to the floor. Repeat on the left.

STANDING CRESCENT POSE

MASTERS OF MINDFULNESS

Fungi can remind us that change, healing and growth all take time. With our relatively short lifespans and our tendency to separate ourselves from nature, we humans want things to happen immediately. We want it to be time to plant seeds now, even though it is still late winter. Then we want the plants to grow, bloom and fruit. As they grow hidden from our eyes in mysterious processes, the slow-growing bodies of fungi – perhaps more than other beings in the garden – remind us that we need to allow time for ourselves to grow and evolve. Sometimes we have to let things sit awhile as the threads of transformation do their work.

Curiously, when we become present to the moment, mindful of existing right now, we step gently out of our impatience and hurry. Perhaps mushrooms are masters of mindfulness. Certainly they are not wrapped up in their minds, stressing about what particle of cellulose to deconstruct next. Fungi, and plants too, can become teachers, showing us how to be present to what is, and to allow changes to happen in the natural flow of time.

Fungi teach us about balance, about interconnection and about the strength of diversity. They strengthen the garden and the forest, and they may prove to be one of the keys to a sustainable future. Researchers are very interested in fungi's potential in the field of medicine, especially in regards to cancer care. Certain fungi are able to remediate toxically polluted sites. A team of designers have created ways to grow leather and wood substitutes out of mushrooms, which costs less and is more sustainable than cattle farming or cutting down trees for lumber. Everywhere they grow, fungi produce rich soil, a gift to gardeners. Next time you see them coming up in your garden, send them thanks, for they are likely creating health in the soil.

SEED DISPERSAL

There are many resourceful ways a plant can form to aid the dispersal of the seed in the most efficient way. The plant adapts into shapes and sizes that achieve the maximum chances of dispersal and this is dependent on where the plant likes to grow.

Below are a few ways that a seed can travel some distance from the parent plant to its new growing place.

WIND

Some seeds develop a shape that will enable them to be carried by the wind, such as dandelion parachutes, which have feathery hairs that help them travel long distances. Maple keys, which have developed propeller-like wings, spin as they fall from the tree and can be taken off by the wind. And some flowers, such as red campion, transform into a pepper-pot form that releases the seeds from small holes when the wind blows the stem.

WATER

Plants that grow by the water rely on water to carry seeds to new locations, such as the palm with its floating coconut fruits or sea kale (*Crambe maritima*). They can travel long distances this way and will either germinate in the water or when they eventually become lodged in a muddy bank.

EXPLOSIVE

As they dry, some plant pods will open explosively and expel their seeds – plants from the Leguminosae family, for example, like gorse and pea. As the pods are drying, a tension forms in the wall of the pod, which eventually releases like a tight spring and flicks away the seeds.

HITCHHIKING

Some seeds have developed sticky hooks or spines, which attach to passing animals or humans and hitch a ride for great distances – for example, burdock and goose grass.

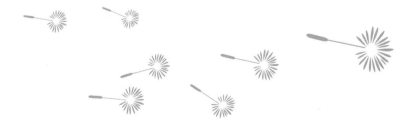

MINDFUL MAKING

Being a maker can be as joyful as using our hands to create something. But by connecting our head and heart to the process, through mindful thoughts, we can tap into a richer depth of our creative practice. The act of joining hands, heart and head together creates something bigger than ourselves, while also allowing us to better understand ourselves. The things we make with our hands have the power to create change in our minds and our hearts.

Being a maker at heart is often about more than the act of using your hands to make something: deep in ourselves, there seems to be an underlying sense of why we make something, how we make it and the connections we create through the journey.

JOURNALLING

SUSTAINING THE WRITER

With the commitment we've made to our writing comes the need to sustain and care for the writer in us. Here are six 'areas of maintenance' that need regular attention.

1. We are writers, and need to write. We feel unsettled if we leave too much time between writing sessions. Getting back to it helps us feel fine again.

2. We need our voice to be heard, so we connect with our inner voice every day.

3. We'll be cheered and encouraged by the endorphins provided by physical movement, so let's take regular exercise.

4. We can be helped and inspired by our own writing talisman. Let's find an artefact or small object that reminds us of that writer in us, and keep it in a pocket or on our desk.

5. We are part of nature, so let's take our senses into nature every day, even if just to feel the air and see the sky.

6. We need a 'stepping back' time when we are aware, without judgement, of our life's realities, and of creativity as an essential part of that life. So let's give ourselves that time every day.

UNDER PATCHING

Under patching is a great method for repairing your clothes. It involves adding a patch to the inside of a garment where the hole or rip is, and then creating different stitch designs over the patch. Bear in mind that your patches will receive considerable wear and tear, so choose durable fabrics where possible. This is a wonderful activity to embrace conscious creativity: if you don't have a set pattern in mind, start adding stitches to the edge of the and patch and see where they take you.

TOOLS AND MATERIALS

- a garment needing repair
- patch of fabric, a good 5cm (2in) larger all round than the hole that needs mending
- safety pins or basting spray
- quilting thread or sewing thread, depending on the weight of the fabric you are mending
- needle
- scissors

METHOD

1. Turn the garment inside out and lay the area that needs mending flat.

2. Place your patch face down over the hole, ensuring that the patch extends by at least 5cm (2in) all the way around the hole. If the area around the hole is worn thin, ensure the patch goes well beyond these worn areas.

3. Secure in place with safety pins or large basting stitches around the edges. If you have temporary spray adhesive for basting, spray it onto the right side of the patch and stick it in place.

4. Turn the garment right side out again.

5. Mark out your design on the garment, covering the whole patched area. Just remember that the denser the stitching, the stronger the mend, so keep your stitches relatively close together.

6. Once you are ready to stitch your design, thread your needle, bring it through from the back and begin stitching.

7. When you have finished, knot the thread on the back and trim the tail. Turn the garment inside out again and if there are any unstitched areas of the patch, you can trim these away. Remove the safety pins or basting stitches, if used. Turn right side out again and your garment is ready to wear.

KINGDOM OF FUNGI

Throughout the soil, snaking their way through rotting logs, are the hidden wizards of the natural world. Mycelium, the lacing white strands produced by some species of fungi, transform organic matter into rich, nourishing humus. Gardeners are beginning to learn what forests have known for millennia – that rich soil comes largely from the work of fungi – and are learning to invite them into the garden instead of trying to destroy them. While it is true that some fungi are responsible for plant diseases like rusts, mildews and tree fungus, most fungi in the garden are beneficial. Mushrooms and mycelium cycle carbon, taking it out of plant matter and into the soil. They create soil by breaking down wood and other fibres into fluffy dark humus. Certain fungi even help protect plants from consumption by insects and herbivores.

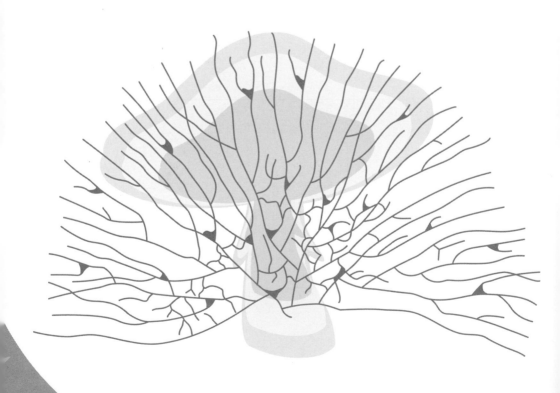

TUNING INTO FUNGI

Mycelium grows from some types of fungi, and these inconspicuous tendrils do more than just break down plant matter. They also form part of nature's Internet. By connecting into the network of mycelium, plant roots are actually able to communicate via chemical signals to other plants. This communication network covers large distances and can link different species together. The network helps plants share nutrients and builds their immune systems by helping to fight off pathogens. In our information age, we could potentially learn a lot from the fungi, who perfected the information highway long ago.

The mindful gardener knows to sit and listen, to learn from this kingdom of fungi, mushrooms and mycelium. What do the travelling strands of white tell us about cycles of life? One thing to be learnt from fungi is that they are not all the same, and the different types have different functions. Some break down plant lignin while others transform cellulose. Another kind of fungi just recently discovered, called endophytic fungi, live in between plant cells and protect plants from herbivores and drought. The world of fungi is vast and varied, and we are beginners in understanding it. This sings to the value of diversity, and is a reminder to listen to the varied voices of others, especially those different from what we are used to.

HARVESTING SEEDS

The best way of building up your seed collection is to harvest them directly from plants. When you collect from the wild you are going straight to the source – it tells you the conditions that plant will thrive in, how big it grows, when it flowers, and when it sets seed.

THE BEST TIME

Harvest seeds when the flower has died and the pod is ripe and swollen. Sometimes the petals are absent or have died and turned brown or black. It varies from plant to plant and happens throughout the summer and into the autumn months. If you collect the seeds just before they would disperse naturally, you know they will be ripe. Read the plant profiles to find out when the plant sets seed.

THE RIGHT WAY

This varies and is dependent on the type of fruit. With red campion, for example, the seeds are wind-dispersed and the openings appear as the seed pod dries; you can therefore collect the seed just before the openings appear in the pod. This will enable you to collect larger numbers of seed. If you are a keen collector, take the following whenever you go for a country walk:

- Camera
- Pencil or Pen
- Paper Bags
- Secateurs or Scissors
- String

METHOD

1. Photograph the plant you harvest from.

2. Label each bag even if you don't know what the plant is. Note down distinctive features to help identify your crop when you get home – for example 'blue thistle-like flowers but no spikes on leaves'.

3. Cut the seed pod/head off, leaving at least 20cm (7¾in) of stem if possible.

4. Place in the labelled paper bag with the pods facing down. When you have a good bunch of about 20 stems, tie the bag around the stems.

5. Store the bags suspended anywhere that is dry and warm, like a kitchen or airing cupboard.

6. Time taken for the pods to be dry enough to release the seeds into the bag also varies from plant to plant; it can take a number of weeks before the seeds are released.

7. Check every now and then by looking inside the bag to see if the pods have dried. You can often hear them falling.

TIP

When you harvest seeds don't be greedy; leave some seed heads behind for the birds to feed on and for future plants to grow.

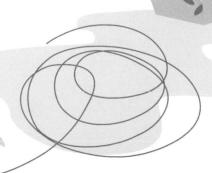

MAKE YOUR OWN SEEDBANK

SEPARATING THE SEEDS FROM THE CHAFF

Once your seed pods or seed heads are dry, the seeds are ready to be separated from all the bits of plant debris that surround them – this is called the chaff. It can be quite tricky, and being prepared with a clear space and the right tools is a good way to start. There are a few ways of getting seeds from the pod and it depends on the plant. Wind-dispersed seeds are released from the pods by gently tapping against a bowl or some paper. Some wind-dispersed pods have chambers, which seeds will hide in and will need to be gently crushed in a sieve over a bowl; the sieve will catch the chaff and allow the seed to fall through. Clustered seed heads, like marigolds, should be pinched apart once they have dried.

TOOLS AND MATERIALS

- Bags of dried seeds (see pages 284–285)
- Newspaper
- Bowl
- Sieve
- Tweezers
- Paper or card container
- Airtight jar
- Pen or pencil
- Label

METHOD

1. Take down your bags, plant by plant (so as not to mix up the seeds).

2. Lay out the newspaper on a table or the floor and place the bowl on top.

3. Place the sieve over the bowl.

4. Tear open the bag, leaving the corners intact as seeds may have collected there.

5. Remove the stems and place them on the newspaper.

6. Tip the remaining seeds from the bag into the sieve to separate the chaff.

7. Tweezer any remaining seeds out of tricky corners.

8. Dry the seeds for a couple of days in a paper or card container.

9. Place in an airtight jar and label it for easy identification.

10. Store in a cool, dry and dark place. Correct storage can lengthen the lives of seeds considerably.

BUILD CONFIDENCE

Try this, anytime, anywhere, when you need an instant confidence boost. As you stand, lengthen your spine and relax your shoulders. Feel the weight drop into your feet and imagine you're supported by an enormous oak tree. Its trunk keeps you upright and gives you strength and confidence. You lean against the bark and feel the warm energy seeping beneath your skin. Your feet are anchored to the floor, by roots that grow from each sole and spread deep beneath the earth. You are connected to nature and ready for anything!

Good posture generates positive energy. It affects the way we think and feel and allows us to breathe correctly, which in turn floods the system with oxygen, providing focus and clarity.

I am perfect as I am.

I am nurtured by nature.

Magic lives in my soul.

I give love, I receive
love, I am love.

CATCHING THE ELUSIVE SCENT

The practice of mindfulness begins by focusing on the breath; for the moment, you let go of any tormenting baggage in the mind – anxious thoughts from yesterday, nagging worries about tomorrow – and relax into the body and its life-giving breath. You let the in-breath gently fill the lungs, hold it for a moment and then allow it to flow out again. You do it in your own time and to your own rhythm, without forcing the air either way. In this way, we begin to be more alert, awake and aware. And with the breath comes that elusive scent. Sniff too hard and it escapes you; wait, breathe gently and you may catch it again. The olfactory system is one of the oldest sensory parts of the brain, evolved in mammals to help in the detection of food and the discernment of poison (how clever of evolution to locate the nose so close to the mouth!). For most of us, however, it has become a deadened sense; we don't rely on it for any useful information, and apart from the delight that comes with the first smell of the morning's coffee or the disgust with the traffic fumes of the city, we neglect what it has to tell us.

Despite this elusiveness, there are smells that momentarily overpower us with memory. The smell of tar takes us back to the garden gate when we were three years old, watching men mend the road; the smell of new-mown hay transports us to happy summers in childhood. We step into the carriage of a train and are suddenly transported we know not where by the faintest of smells: 'I have been here before! When? Where was I when I last caught that familiar, but long forgotten, odour?' The timelessness of the experience can be very strange as we search in our thoughts to locate its origins. Then it is gone, lost perhaps like a hint of honeysuckle on the night air. We are left wondering.

NOVEMBER

Time to reflect. Crafting, handwork and the art of slow stitch remind us to appreciate the meditative nature of doing.

THE MAGIC IN MAKING

There is a kind of magic that happens when the raw material of life knits together through the creative act. Our knowledge and experience is like a unique lens through which we filter the felt, experiential and unfathomable aspects of the world we exist in. Quite often we don't even realize the depth of what comes out of us, but through the mindful practice of art we can listen carefully enough to hear, or perhaps more accurately see, the voice within our tangible products of creation, and the voice of others.

Reading the visual language of art is as complicated as the act of creation itself. Art is not spelt out for us in literal terms, and when we try to interpret it with such concrete methods we often find that words fall short. There is a whole academic and historical discipline based on the rich discussion and interpretation of artworks and the methods thought best to understand them. The interpretation of art, both our own and that of others, is also notoriously individual. Science tells us that the neuroplasticity of our brains means that no two minds are wired the same. Each web of neurons and synaptic connections are woven so very uniquely that in both the creation and appreciation of art there must be infinite possibilities.

Yet, there are times when we stand before an artwork and it speaks to us. Sometimes it is our own work and other times it is the expression of another, but in these instances of resonance there is an opportunity to dwell deeply within the experience and gain great insight.

ART THAT SPEAKS TO US

Quite often the response we have to an artwork is an aesthetic one. We feel and respond to art bodily, with senses that reach far beyond the visual. Our skin prickles, our hearts sing or our throats constrict. Mindfully experiencing this physical response by being present in our bodies and observing how they react in the viewing, we can pinpoint which part of the body is moved by the work. As we turn our mental attention inwards, we may feel emotions bubble up or have memories flash through us.

Taking the time to pointedly and quietly dwell with art can be enlightening. All too often, we can paint an artwork, not knowing what it is about or having any intention for the work's meaning. But in dwelling with the work after its completion, its meaning and the origin of its meaning becomes clear. It is a marvellous thing to realize that our creative production can come from a place entirely different from planning and control, and even more fascinating to realize that this is also the place that our best art comes from. The call and response of art can be felt and found in the here and now.

A YOGA SEQUENCE TO BALANCE YOUR CHAKRAS

DURATION: 10–15 minutes
YOGA STYLE: Classical Hatha
GOOD FOR: Balancing the Chakras, invigorating the pranic system, releasing energetic blockage

This Hatha yoga sequence can release blockages and stagnant energy from your chakras, which helps prana (your vital life-force energy) to flow properly. You may find that clearing your chakras brings other benefits, such as clarity of mind, emotional balance or a flow of creativity.

Hold the postures for 5–10 breaths (on each side when the pose is done on the left and right legs). For the sacral chakra pose, perform the variation of Warrior II, which is Reverse Warrior. The throat chakra pose is comprised of 2 postures: Shoulder Stand and Fish Pose. Fish acts as counter pose to Shoulder Stand and should always follow this strong posture. If Shoulder Stand is too strong for you or is contraindicated due to neck issues, perform Fish Pose alone for the throat chakra.

End your practice by allowing the prana to flow around your energetic system.

1. GARLAND POSE

2. REVERSE WARRIOR

3. COBRA POSE

4. BOW POSE

5. SUPPORTED
SHOULDER STAND

6. FISH POSE

7. CHILD'S POSE

8. RABBIT POSE

FIFTY WORDS FOR RAIN

Rainstorms come in many different flavours. There is light, misty rain like you find in a cloud forest. Pounding rain that strips leaves off the trees. A gentle rain you know will last all day, or even for several days. Rain can come in bursts just enough to wet the pavement and fill the air with petrichor, then blow past. Summer rain clears the air and makes fat droplets in the dust. Moss-creating rain is somewhere between mist and gentle rain. Early winter rain sinks into your bones and urges you to curl up with a book instead of going outside. What kind of rain do you love?

Often when it rains, you feel calmer and more settled. Partly this is because of low pressure. While life doesn't stop for rain, we get a sort of reprieve from going and doing so much when wet stuff is falling from the sky. Rain reflects the soul of an introvert, yin and quiet. As sky and Earth are united through water, we come gently into ourselves. Rain is an invitation for mindfulness.

Listening to rain can be a simple meditation. Next time it rains, take time to become present through the sound of the rain. Hear it patter on the window or pound on the roof. Let your breath move in and out of your lungs. Can you feel more moisture in the air? You are breathing in water from some other place on Earth. You are here now, in this intersection of time and space, weather and breath. Close your eyes and let the sound become you. Water is life. You are life. All is one.

MINDFUL WALKING

The thing to remember about mindfulness is that it is completely natural, something we often practise without even trying. When alert and absorbed in weeding the garden, cooking a meal, painting a picture or enjoying the fresh air and landscape on a country walk, we may already be in a mindful state – consciously involved, here and now, in a fulfilling activity. Such moments may be rare in our daily lives, for our living experience is often cluttered with a background noise of worries and anxieties, self-doubts, stress and uncertainties – but those moments do not have to be rare. By recognizing and savouring the quality of mindfulness, we can learn to foster it and live in peace in the present moment, anywhere.

The principal mindfulness exercise involves our breathing. We depend for our existence upon the invisible life-giving oxygen in the air – five minutes or so without breathing and we are dead, and yet most of the time we give it such little thought. For this exercise, we should be comfortable, standing or sitting, holding the back straight but without strain, not slumped, and with the shoulders open. Nothing should be forced; breathe gently and our bodies will tell us how much air we need. Then we simply watch our breathing, feeling the in-breath as the air flows in, opening our lungs, following the out-breath as our lungs deflate. By focusing on this simple activity, we find that our mind has stopped roaming about and our bodies begin to experience calm.

FINDING OUR RHYTHM

We can also practise mindfulness while walking, coordinating our breathing with the regular swing of our limbs. Again, nothing should be forced; simply get into a comfortable rhythm and become aware of how the breath comes and goes. We are all built differently and have to find our own way into what instinctively feels right and easy. The Zen Buddhist master Thich Nhat Hanh has some recommendations in his little book *How to Walk*; he considers how to enjoy walking through crowds in a busy city or in an airport and how to climb stairs. He suggests that we should begin by taking two steps for the in-breath and three steps for the out-breath – or, if we find it easier, three steps and five steps. The numbers will be reduced when climbing a hill. We listen to our bodies and adapt, each of us finding our own natural rhythm.

MINDFUL BREATHING AND MINDFUL WALKING

Mindful breathing and mindful walking are the basis for our further exploration of the way in which we relate to the world we inhabit and, contemplate our place in the living ecosystem, our connections to other creatures. We feel the earth beneath our feet and the steady pull of the gravity of the planet – particularly when toiling uphill. By becoming more aware of our bodies in the present moment, we have located a strong place from which to become more conscious and appreciative of our surroundings.

THE MAGICIAN: A BEDTIME MEDITATION FOR INNER STRENGTH

You are sitting at the top of a mountain. A blanket of stars rests above your head, and the night is rich with mystery. You can see shapes in the distance, the outline of other mountains huddled together, and above them the full moon glows. You take a deep breath in and draw the cool air down into your lungs. As you exhale, you pour any fears into this outward breath. Peace permeates your being.

Sitting crossed legged, rooted to the spot, you feel safe and secure. From this vantage point you can see for miles around. Being so high up, so free, makes you feel in control and you take another deep breath, drinking in the power of this place. A tiny flame, a pinprick of light, sparks inside your belly, and it grows with every breath you take. The warmth spreads as the fire ignites, and you feel infused with strength. The moon turns her attention to you, bathing you in her luminescent stare. You smile and at your very core, something solidifies.

'I embrace my power', you say.

Then, holding your hands out, you focus and hone your intent upon the space at your feet, as the fire within sizzles. Where once there was nothing but dry earth, there now sits a small fire; a place to warm your soul. You are not surprised by this show of power. You know you can do anything you set your mind to.

Slowly rising, you turn, arms outstretched. You lift your face to the moon and spin, and as you do, the fire spreads in a perfect circle around you. This ring of flames provides protection and a sacred space where you can access your inner strength.

'I am strong', you shout into the night.

As if in response, your words echo back.

'I am strong, strong, strong...'

Once more you sit in the centre of the circle you have created. The flames surge upwards, and the wall of fire cocoons you, making you feel even more empowered. You place your hands flat upon the dusty terrain. A tingle vibrates in the middle of each palm, and then as you lift them upwards, a tiny sapling springs to life. It bursts from this brittle landscape pushing its head towards the stars, and you marvel at the new life. The shoots twine around your fingers, and you feel earth energy mingle with your own essence.

It holds you firm and keeps you safe.

It defines your strength.

You take a gulp of refreshing air and feel your stomach swell. As you exhale, a stream of white light pours from your lips, it twists and turns until it forms a shape, a symbol to represent your personal power. The symbol hovers in the night sky above your head; a beacon of your strength for all the world to see.

COOL-SEASON GARDEN

The greens from a hoop house or cold frame are unlike any you will buy at the store, and even different from spring garden greens. Winter veggies are tough. Their cell walls are strong against the cold, able to survive cycles of freezing and thawing. Their roots hold strong under the soil, protected just enough to stay alive. The leaves are dark green, and tend to be small and dense. They match the feeling inside us in winter: sturdy, rooted, biding time till spring.

The cool-season garden suggests, however, that while winter is a time of dormancy and rest, with a little shelter there can still be life and growth. Sometimes we can be like dandelions growing in cracks – nothing can hold us back; we are diamonds in the rough. But after a while, without support, we wither and stop growing. We need a kind soul to bring us a little water, a little encouragement. We are more like tender perennials than hardy dandelions. When our needs are heard and respected, when we are given just a little boost of natural fertilizer at the right time, we can flourish.

THE WINTER TUNNEL OF LIFE

At times, it feels like our own ground is frozen solid and we can't garner enough nutrients to keep going, but whether we're talking pot size to root ball or frozen ground beneath a winter tunnel, what it all amounts to is that we need the right ground to support us, the right climate to keep us going. Gardening in any season reminds us that the spark lives in us at all times, but we need that call, that request, that support to pull us where we need to go. Then, when the time is right, we can flourish.

When you do not know what is waiting to unfold and grow, the trick is to go into the silence of the winter tunnel. Listen to the stillness. Don't direct or label or force, just listen. In stillness and silence sometimes what we need to hear is revealed. Then we must let it germinate in its own time.

BUILD INNER STRENGTH

Think of a time when you achieved something that you're proud of. This could be passing an exam, getting a new job or promotion, or even something practical like decorating your home.

Imagine you are watching a film of the experience in your mind and when you reach the moment of victory, freeze the frame and press your index finger and thumb together in a pinching motion.

Say out loud or in your head 'I can do anything I set my mind to'. Repeat this process every day for a week to re-enforce the action and thought pattern. Whenever you need extra reserves of strength and determination, pinch your index finger and thumb together, and you'll be instantly reminded of your awesomeness!

I am victorious in all things.

The power of my mind is enough.

I always reach my destination.

Endurance is my superpower.

NOURISHING OURSELVES

Modern society seems intent on being busy, where there isn't time to stop for a moment and look up from our work, chores or extra-curricular activities. People rush around, working dedicatedly on finishing work, attending to projects or pleasing other people and meeting their needs. Yet studies and reports – and simple conversations with others – show us that this is creating anxiety, illness, depression and a sense of overwhelm that our community doesn't know how to deal with, and our health departments aren't equipped for. It is hard to step outside our busy lives for long enough to recognize that we too are feeling overwhelmed by our to-do lists and our keeping up with appearances, by our efforts to stay on track with living the fullness of life that we aspire to. It sometimes seems easier to not face our stress, to push it away, but that only contributes to making it worse.

By scheduling the time and space for a hobby or a break into our days, even just once a week, we are giving ourselves permission to seek the quiet that we so desperately need yet often don't even realize we're longing for. Making a cup of coffee and settling down outside to listen to birds and observe our surroundings for a small moment, gives space for our busy brains to stop whirling, and concentrate on other things.

Our practice of yoga, meditation or our daily making projects can guide us in our everyday experiences. The gentle reminders to nourish our body, to reassess our posture and give our minds quiet space means these practices become almost like second nature to us, and can be taken into our busy workplaces, or into the chaos of family life.

It can change our outlook on our whole life. Rather than endlessly wanting to be somewhere else or someone else, we can stop and appreciate where we are right now. Our seasons of self will continue to flow; it is up to us to enjoy being fully present in each stage.

THE PLEAIDES CLUSTER

Taurus, one of the Zodiac constellations, is a large, prominent fixture in the later part of the year. Within the area of the constellation is the Pleiades cluster, or 'Seven Sisters' (M45), best viewed in November of each year. Despite the name, there are actually six stars visible to the naked eye, and if you look through binoculars or a telescope you'll find hundreds of stars sparkling like diamonds.

FINDING AWE & BEAUTY

Gazing up at the sky on a really dark night is mesmerizing: pitch dark from horizon to horizon, punctuated by thousands of points of twinkling lights, like tiny jewels on a silk cloth. And when you see something like the Pleiades in a telescope for the first time, you can't fail to be awestruck. Whether we know the science behind what we're looking at or not, the intrinsic beauty of the night sky remains unchanged. It's a source of inspiration, fascination and wonder. The next time you look up, take a moment to allow the exquisite splendour of the starscape to capture your eyes and your heart.

MINDFUL EATING,
MINDFUL MEALTIMES

Food is too important to be rushed so let's make a conscious decision to set aside our mealtimes to truly savour and appreciate it. We may then be more deeply nourished by it and wrapped in an uplifting sense of gratitude for all it represents.

When the moment for a meal arrives, there comes an opportunity to celebrate the sustaining wonder of replenishment in a very direct way. Even before the meal has begun, much work and thought has gone into creating the food we eat, from growing, harvesting, transporting, shopping to careful cooking. All these aspects can be brought into focus when we choose to make our mealtimes mindful.

A meal is almost always a source of natural and frequent joy. For food not to bring joy it needs to be either very bad, or the eater unwell in some way that impoverishes their normal instinctual delight.
The general robustness of our love of food and the usual frequency of mealtimes make breakfast, lunch or supper perfect moments to practise mindfulness. Mindful eating could become a regular thing, or something you do once a day – or perhaps just for ten minutes now and then.

To begin with, make sure that you have set aside a quiet, undisturbed
place in which to enjoy your meal. Set aside all your electronic
paraphernalia: no ear plugs feeding you with music or news.
Mobile turned off. Kitchen TV, off. Once you have served yourself,
notice how one dish complements another. Enjoy the colours, sometimes
matching and muted, other times striking with dramatic contrasts of
colour. Take in the aromas of the food as they waft up to your nose.
Eat slowly, enjoying and appreciating the food. Tune into
the taste and texture and the way each morsel transforms in your
mouth. As you swallow, feel it travelling into your body and becoming
part of your strength, no longer a separate entity but part of your very
being. Between mouthfuls, put down your utensils and allow your hands
to relax so you can concentrate on the sensations in your mouth. Be in
no hurry to take another bite before the first is finished.

Mindful eating is an exercise not only in reaffirming the simple
satisfaction of mealtimes, it also provides an opportunity to engage
in gratefulness, which is an attitude to life that has been shown to
promote greater happiness. Rather than focusing on what we have not,
we are thankful for what we have.

THE HABIT OF
MINDFUL BREATHING

Breathing into the full capacity of your lungs is the foundation of
meditation and yoga, but it can also be practised through your daily
making. Using your creative work as the reminder for slow and deep
breathing will help guide you towards a healthier body and mind. By
routinely incorporating deep breathing into your making activities,
it can become a habitual part of your creative practice and your life.

Actively focusing on your breath is the first step, noticing when you are
breathing deeply or only taking shallow breaths. The quality of your
breathing can change depending on what your creative practice is, but
sitting up straight while you work helps with better breathing (not to
mention posture and back problems). Sitting hunched over your potter's
wheel or sewing machine or curled up awkwardly with your crochet
isn't ideal for long periods of making or for deep breathing. Setting
up your workspace carefully, such as adjusting your chair and table
height, makes a difference to the ease with which your body will cope
with extended periods of making. And while it might not be practical to
always sit straight or mindfully, it's possible to keep remembering to
tend to your posture, with practice.

OBSERVING THE RHYTHM OF THE SKIES

Day by day, the rising time of each star shifts ever so slightly, as does the time of the sunrise and sunset. That shift is very precise – so much so that we have to add a leap second to our clocks every few years. The Sun and moon follow their own rhythms, and rarer events such as meteor showers and eclipses add a certain syncopation to the heavenly beat. Observation of the sky was first undertaken as a way of recording its rhythms and cycles, in order to create a calendar. In ancient times, astronomers were priests, and astronomical calculations were often preciously guarded secrets. In ancient China, the main responsibility of political power was to keep the Earth in harmony with the sky. This so-called 'Mandate of Heaven' meant that astronomers had influence over daily life as well as major political strategies. In ancient Greece, a solar eclipse around the year 600 BCE was predicted by the philosopher Thales and was interpreted as an omen. It interrupted a battle between the Medes and the Lydians and brought it to a truce. In many cultures, being able to predict astronomical events meant power. The Atharva Veda, a collection of hymns written in India around 1500 BCE, was one of the earliest texts that described rituals based on astronomical knowledge. Texts like this gave the rulers power to know exactly the right day to perform the right ritual to the right god to ensure they achieved their goal, whether that was winning a battle, fathering a son or making sure enough rain fell to water the crops.

IN TUNE WITH NATURE, AND OURSELVES

For aeons and aeons, humans and animals have lived by the cycles of nature. Our bodies have evolved to be incredibly well tuned into them. How do migrating birds such as swallows know to leave Africa and return to northern Europe in spring? How do they navigate? They do it because they are in tune with and sensitive to the world around them. These days, we humans have found ways of disconnecting from almost every one of these natural cycles. But what price do we pay for losing touch with the world's natural rhythms?

A keen stargazer is always in touch with the astronomical cycles. Observing the rhythms of the sky helps reconnect us to those of the whole natural world, and being aware of these helps us to notice our own personal rhythms, too. Some people have a lower mood in the winter when the Sun is elusive, while others find their low mood always comes on a Monday morning. Some people believe their behaviour or events in their lives are linked to the location of the Sun in particular constellations. The Buddha taught us that all things change. If we can bring attention to our inner rhythms with an attitude of non-judgement and acceptance, we can flow along with the outer rhythms of Earth and the stars more gracefully and sensitively.

WINTER

DECEMBER

JANUARY

FEBRUARY

WINTER PLAYLIST

· *We Are All Made of Stars* – Moby

· *Flowers In December* – Mazzy Star

· *Winter Fields* – Bat For Lashes

· *A Hazy Shade of Winter* – Simon & Garfunkel

· *The Blizzard* – Camera Obscura

· *White Winter Hymnal* – Fleet Foxes

· *Goodbye England (Covered In Snow)*
  – Laura Marling

*Now is my time to rest, reflect
and renew my spirit.*

I am nature and nature is me.

*I accept I am imperfect
and love that I am.*

DECEMBER

Time to rejoice. Celebrations and festivities mark the year that's passed and unite life experiences all over the world.

CREATING TIME

Finding space to fit our creative work around our life, jobs, families and downtime can be a little stressful at times. Either we want to rush everything else to give ourselves as much time with our making tools as possible, or we feel guilty when we take time away from others to fulfil our own creative needs. It doesn't seem to make a lot of difference whether you are a full-time professional, occasional hobbyist or somewhere in between. The time and space for our creative work doesn't just magically appear, and we must create a space for ourselves.

It seems vital that rather than accepting the negatives of having too little time and being pulled away from our need for making, we should instead approach time peaceably, actively making room in our lives for what matters to us. The world seems ever busier, with time spinning away from us, and we cannot afford to lose focus and drift off mindlessly or we may one day look back and wonder where our days went. Being busy without purpose is not a hallmark of importance, but rather an indication that we are not paying attention to our days in a thoughtful, considered way. Letting work or external commitments drag us away from what we want to do, leaving us ragged and rundown, gives little space for our making or our commitment to a slower, simpler way of living. Being busy is sometimes a resistance to other things, and an indication that you need to slow time down in a meaningful manner.

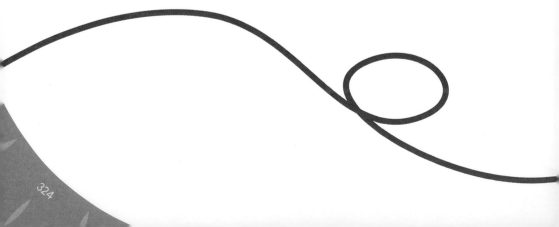

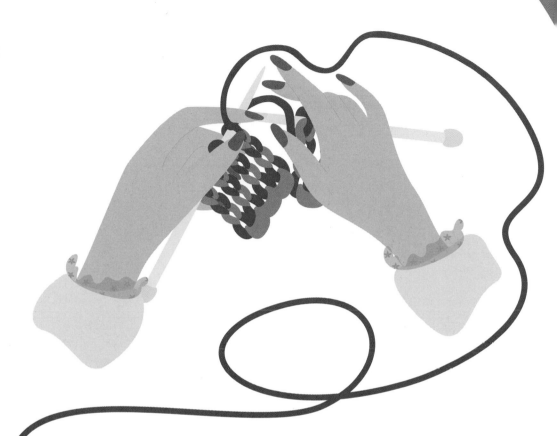

As a traditional Zen saying goes, 'You should sit in meditation for 20 minutes a day – unless you're too busy, then you should sit for an hour.'

Being mindful in our creative practice, by actively choosing to prioritize the space and time for ourselves, brings attention to our internal core. Focusing on even just one thing makes us slow down a little from the rush of everyday life. Mindful making is about more than stitching or knitting something beautiful; it is about learning how to bring that focus or feel of attention to something (the stitch work, the pattern) in our daily lives.

MOVEMENT

MELTING HEART POSE
Anahatasana

DURATION: 1–2 minutes
YOGA STYLE: Yin yoga
GOOD FOR: Opening your heart, restorative

Begin on your hands and knees. Walk your hands forwards to bring your chest closer to the mat. Keep your hips stacked above your knees and your arms shoulder-width apart, palms on the mat. Rest your forehead on the mat. To exit, carefully walk your hands back to all fours. Come into a Child's Pose as a counter posture.

MODIFICATIONS

If you have shoulder issues, bend your elbows away from each other, and move your hands towards each other. If your forehead does not reach the mat, rest your forehead on a block or blanket.

VARIATION: DEEPEN THE STRETCH (INTERMEDIATE)

If you have enough flexibility and no neck issues, rest the chest and chin on the mat.

MELTING HEART POSE

ENTERING SILENCE

For those living in urban areas, it is hard to find quiet. There is the constant background rumble of traffic, sirens in the distance and the whine of aeroplanes overhead. For some, the idea of being in silence is so uncomfortable that they make sure it never happens by always having the television or radio on or music playing in the background. For others that live in the countryside, the silence at nighttime can be so complete that you can hear a pin drop.

Unlike our eyes, which we can close against distractions, we cannot close our ears. Mindfulness is therefore often practised in silence. Of course, it is almost never totally silent, but in trying to stay as quiet as possible without any unnecessary talking we minimize any distractions for ourselves and others and help create an atmosphere of space and calm. Staying quiet gives us a chance to feel, to listen and observe the incessant internal chatter – the constant commentary, judgements and reflections on what is going on. However, as much as we might want to, it is not possible to forcibly quieten or clear the mind.

Mindfulness is not about how busy or calm the mind is, it is about how we relate to our thoughts. By learning how to accept our mind-state just as it is, things will eventually quieten down, just like a jug of swirling water will eventually settle if you give it time.

Being in silence allows us the space to notice things we might otherwise miss – the wind in the trees, the sparkle of sunlight through the water glass, the tick of the clock or the twinkle of the stars. Looking up at the night sky is a quiet activity. The world is stiller at nighttime, and the sky itself makes its slow wheeling procession without a single sound.

FINDING THE HIDDEN SILENCE

Right now, as you read this, take a moment to tune into your sense of hearing. Just listen for a few moments. Try not to label or judge the sounds you hear; just open your awareness to the soundscape around you. Are there any subtler sounds that perhaps take a few minutes to become obvious? Sounds are like thoughts: some are fleeting, while some arise and pass more slowly; some are loud, some quiet; some are pleasurable and compelling, some ugly and aversive.

Now see if you can find the silence underlying the sounds. Take your time. It is always there, like the blue sky is always there behind the clouds. It is there on a busy station platform at rush hour behind all the hubbub and clatter. It is still there when your mind is racing at a million miles an hour with all those to-do lists and ideas. A very traditional image is that of the storm on the ocean. It doesn't matter how wild the wind and rain is on the surface, it is always calm and quiet in the water deep below.

CRAFT

KNITTING BASICS

Knitting is such a fulfilling craft: as well as creating something unique, it has mindful properties as well. As you work on your garment, embrace the meditative rhythm of creating the stitches, and breathe.

TOOLS AND EQUIPMENT

- · 1 skein double knit (dk) yarn
- · 1 pair 4.25mm (US6) knitting needles

MAKING A SLIPKNOT

Every piece of knitting begins with a slipknot. The slipknot counts as the first stitch on your needle.

1. Loop your yarn as if to make a knot, leaving a tail of about 10cm (4in) in length.

2. Use the knitting needle tip to catch the yarn inside the loop.

3. Continue by tightening the knot on the needle. This is your slipknot or first stitch.

KNITTED CAST-ON

The knitted cast-on creates a very neat edge to your knitting, and is suitable for most projects. Every stitch is pulled through the previous loop. This gives the cast-on edge extra strength.

1. Make a slipknot, as shown opposite, and hold the needle with the slipknot in your left hand. To knit the first stitch, insert the right-hand (RH) needle through the first stitch (slipknot) from left through to right.

2. Wrap the yarn around the RH tip from right to left (anticlockwise). Pull the new loop through the stitch on the left-hand (LH) needle.

3. Place the stitch back on the LH needle. You now have two stitches.

4. Continue to cast on by inserting the RH needle into the next stitch on the LH needle, wrapping the yarn around the tip of the RH needle and pulling the loop of the wrapped yarn through the stitch with the tip of the RH needle. Then place the stitch on the LH needle. Repeat until you have the required number of stitches.

KNIT STITCH

The knit stitch is one of the basic fundamental stitches used in most knitting patterns. Once you have mastered this stitch, you can work and follow different stitch patterns. It is indicated in patterns as (k).

1. Hold the needle with the cast-on stitches in your left hand.

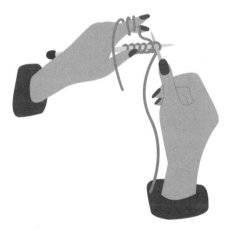

2. Insert the RH needle from left to right through the front of the first stitch on your LH needle.

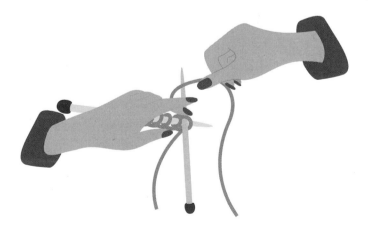

3. Wrap the yarn from left to right over the end of the RH needle. Pull the yarn through the stitch, this will form a new stitch on the RH needle.

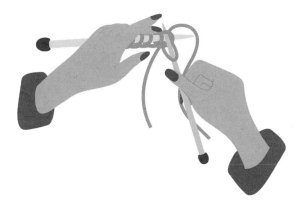

4. Drop the original stitch off the LH needle and keep the new stitch on the RH needle. Repeat steps 1 to 3 until all stitches on the LH needle have been worked. Practise the knit stitch until you can produce a good square swatch.

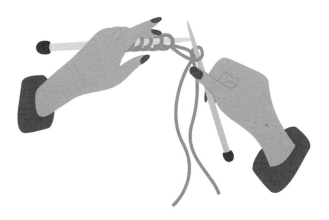

A SENSE OF PLACE

Home is a very spiritual idea that means something different to everyone. The conventional idea of the perfect home is the imagery of magazines: a beautifully designed and perfectly proportioned space. But the spiritual idea of home is less tangible. The feeling of home can reach us through our eyes, our noses, our taste and touch. For some, it could be invoked by the soft air and lush green hills of the countryside. But for others it could be the smell of freshly baked bread, making a recipe from an old family cookbook, sharing a meal with friends with whom you have a long history.

Our homes help us remain connected with these alternative ideas of belonging, and cities – such treasure troves of experiences – allow us to cultivate those more philosophical interpretations. The more we roam, the more we experience of the world, the greater chance we have of feeling rooted, at one, across a greater number of its landscapes, cultures, people. Our shells may be small, but we are the adventurers who are free to taste all of the city's pleasures.

TAP INTO YOUR INNER PEACE

Find an inner well of peace with this exercise, which instils serenity throughout the day.

Start by putting a stop to internal chatter. Every time a negative thought or criticism arises in your mind say 'Stop!' out loud or in your head.

Next, turn your attention to the way you are breathing. Slow down the rhythm by counting to four, slowly, as you breathe in and out, then extend each breath by one count. Repeat this cycle several times until you feel more relaxed.

When you are ready, say the following mantra, either in your head or out loud if circumstance allows. 'Be still, be calm, be pure, just be'. Think about each part of the mantra and what it means as you say it. Repeat several times, or until you feel calm.

The mantra switches the focus of the mind, taking you away from stressful thought patterns. The gentle repetitive rhythm combined with slow, deep breathing relaxes body and mind.

Serenity lives within me.

There is stillness in
every moment.

The key to tranquillity
is in my heart.

Be still, be calm, be
pure, just be.

FINDING STILLNESS ON THE WAY

Stillness and silence are not always what we may think they are. Stillness can be found in a jostling crowd, and silence is not always simply a lack of sound. Going for a good walk provides ample opportunity to get away from the noisy world, to leave the family (however much loved), workplace or office behind for a moment, and to explore the health-giving balm of silence, to discover what it really is and plumb some of its depths.

NOT ALL SILENCE IS GOLDEN

Our forebears must have taken quietness for granted in the way we tend to take breathing for granted. It was natural for them to hear only the sounds of nature while working, birdsong and the lowing of cattle, the wind and the rain, and to return to a low-lit house with only the crackling of the fire and the sound of conversation to disturb the quiet. Those days, for most of us, have gone. We have to make a conscious effort to treat ourselves to the elusive sound of silence, and to cherish it when we have found it.

Of course, not all silence is golden – there are embarrassed silences when we have 'put a foot in it' and spoken out of turn; tense silences in a fractious marriage; aggressive silences fired at us from troubled teenagers; silences from offended friends. All of these have to be handled mindfully in their own way, requiring wisdom, empathy and experience. The sound of silence we are seeking when setting off for a walk is entirely different; it is an inner thing, and not just an escape from the daily assault on our ears. We are seeking rest, and the chance to rediscover the still centre at the heart of our being.

To achieve this, there is no need to find a spot where there is a total lack of noise, where all we can hear is the numbing sound of the blood rushing through our heads. That sort of silence can be torture – and is horribly used as such in some totalitarian regimes. The silence we yearn for is achieved when external sounds – the wind in the trees, a distant dog barking – enhance rather than diminish our own sense of quietness. We have left behind us for a moment the noisy turmoil of life, and have set off mindfully to rediscover, and reconnect with, ourselves.

WINTER WARMING DRINKING CHOCOLATE

This delicious warming drink is the perfect companion to a cold winter's day. Savour the rich cacao taste as you spend a morning journalling or breathe in the spiced aroma as you reflect on your surroundings.

SERVES 2

INGREDIENTS

- 30g (1oz) raw coconut oil
- 500ml (18fl oz) your favourite raw nut or seed milk
  – I like to use hulled hemp seeds
- 70g (2$^{1}/_{2}$oz) yacon syrup
- 1 tsp mixed spice
- 1cm ($^{1}/_{2}$in) piece fresh ginger, peeled

EQUIPMENT

- bain-marie or dehydrator
- power blender
- glass mixing bowl
- two favourite mugs

TIP
*This drink has
a bitter high-cacao
kick but if you want to
make it sweeter, add
a touch more yacon
syrup.*

METHOD

1. If the coconut oil is too firm to blend, melt it down gently into a soft or runny consistency in a bain-marie or dehydrator.

2. Add the coconut oil to your power blender with all of the other ingredients and blend on full power, using the plunger, until smooth.

3. Pour the mixture into a glass mixing bowl and heat in the bain-marie until warm, stirring frequently. Pour into 2 favourite mugs and enjoy straight away.

THE GARDEN UNDER SNOW

Under a blanket of snow lies a curled emerald dragon, her breath slow but unceasing. She shimmers like a will-o'-the-wisp just outside your line of sight. We gardeners hear her voice in dreams, whispering promises of what the land will bring in a few months' time as she turns over in her hibernation. She is a pulse of life held in the belly of the Earth. We know she will wake in due time. For now, we watch her domain from inside the house holding a steaming mug of tea, waiting.

The winter garden is the garden of hoping for the best. It is a dream garden of huge plump tomatoes and bug-free broccoli, the one we have yet to plant but can nonetheless taste in our mind. It is the garden of plans: in winter we pore over seed catalogues, committing to try something new next spring. We mentally move carrots from one bed to another and wonder if perhaps violets might like that spot under the evergreens. We tap into the dragon's dreams and ask her if there might be somewhere we could tuck another apple tree.

This winter garden of dreams and plans is no less real than the green and growing garden. A blueprint is no less real than a house. When we run our fingers over the pages of a seed catalogue, marvelling at the greens and purples and oranges we have yet to grow, we plant seeds in our own mind, seeds of commitment and dreams. If you have ever had a dream and followed it through, you know how powerful these seeds of the mind and heart can be. This, too, is the garden.

CONTEMPLATING THE GARDEN'S SKELETON

The winter garden covered in snow is a chance to appreciate the slower moving energies of a garden. It gifts us with the opportunity not just to dream and plan; with foliage gone and the ugly stillness of winter covered in soft curves of snow, we can see the garden's bones. This gives us a different perspective that can inform our dreaming. What do the stones and pathways, empty arbours and still birdbaths have to tell you? Can you see how energy flows through your garden and listen to the suggestions that a garden skeleton might offer? These perennial features are the container that holds the more active garden of growing things. In some cases, the stone and wood literally provide the container for our garden, and the fallow earth holds up both the garden and the gardener. The winter pathways and structure are an empty stage, ready to receive the actors and dancers of spring. This, too, is the garden.

THE EVER-TURNING WHEEL

As we move through the seasons and all kinds of weather, we and the garden grow together. In winter, we can find this waiting, this stillness. Here we breathe, and witness as time unfolds. The wheel turns, and the mindful gardener knows to sit with whatever is right now, as well as to welcome dreams. We pack all these discoveries in the wheelbarrow, toting them down the paths of life. We come home to ourselves, as we grow in compassion and understanding. We see our paths intersect with billions of plant and animal beings. We sit with the stillness and the promise, and know that in time the days of spring will come.

FINDING MEANING

One beautiful myth from Japan tells of the Milky Way and how it separates the two brightest stars in the sky. The weaver princess Orihime was the daughter of the Heavenly Emperor Tentei and wove beautiful clothes by the bank of the Tennogawa (literally 'heavenly river', what we call the Milky Way). In a meeting arranged by Tentei, Orihime met Hikoboshi, a cowherd boy who worked on the other bank of the river. They fell in love, got married and forgot their work. Over time the god's clothes ended up in tatters and cows strayed all over heaven. In anger, Tentei separated the lovers across the Tennogawa and turned them into Altair and Vega, two of the brightest stars visible from the northern hemisphere. Tentei allowed the two to meet only on the seventh day of the seventh month, when a flock of magpies would fly up to create a bridge across the Milky Way. This event is celebrated in Japan starting on 7 July in the festival called Tanabata. People write their innermost wishes onto a slip of paper, tie it onto a tree branch, or a twig and place it into a river to be carried off.

YOUR LIFE'S OWN STORYLINES

What about our own stories? People say one of the functions of the brain is to create meaning out of our experiences to help us learn. Out of those meanings come storylines. Some of these are useful, but most are not. They serve to limit and fix us into habits and patterns of thinking. For example, you are told as a seven-year-old that you are not good at art and all your drawings look like paint chaotically flicked onto the page. Because of its emotive charge, this comment turns into a storyline that is played internally again and again through your later childhood until it becomes fixed into a belief: 'I'm bad at art'.

Mindfulness helps us to see things more clearly and objectively. By applying attention to our feelings, emotions and thoughts, with acceptance and without judgement, we start to see these storylines for what they are: just stories. Some traditions use the question 'who am I?' as a focus for meditation and a way of punching through these storylines. Our psyche is like a huge onion, and using that question we start to peel off the layers one by one. Each answer we come up with may be partly true, but it is not the whole truth – there's more. The meaning of the Tanabata myth is one of inner alchemy or transformation that represents the path of self-enquiry. The black and white of the magpies are the yin and yang, and the boy and girl are our inner masculine and feminine sides. Most of us live in this world of opposites: I am a man/woman, happy/sad, tense/relaxed, rich/poor, and so on. The meaning of the word 'yoga' is to unite. Yoga is the practice of bringing together our opposites into a place of oneness. There's no longer me here and the big, bad Universe out there; there's just 'me-Universe'. In Tanabata, the meeting of the lovers and fulfilling of the wish represent the coming together of our being into the oneness of the river of life. In that place where there are no opposites, who are you?

A LEAPING HARE READING LIST

This almanac is made up of extracts from some of the best of Leaping Hare Press's books. To read more of the original writing, follow our reading list.

CONSCIOUS CRAFTS: 20 MINDFUL MAKES TO RECONNECT HEAD, HEART & HANDS

Conscious Crafts: Knitting
Vanessa Koranteng &
Sicgmone Kludje, 2022.

Conscious Crafts: Pottery
Lucy Davidson, 2021.

Conscious Crafts: Quilting
Elli Beaven, 2021.

Conscious Crafts: Whittling
Barn the Spoon, 2022.

MINDFUL THOUGHTS

Mindful Thoughts for Artists:
Finding Flow & Creating Calm
Georgina Hooper, 2020.

Mindful Thoughts for Birdwatchers:
Finding Awareness in Nature
Adam Ford, 2018.

Mindful Thoughts for City Dwellers:
The Joy of Urban Living
Lucy Anna Scott, 2018.

Mindful Thoughts for Cooks:
Nourishing Body & Soul
Julia Ponsonby, 2018.

Mindful thoughts for Cyclists:
Finding Balance on Two Wheels
Nick Moore, 2017.

Mindful Thoughts for Fathers: A
Journey of Loving-kindness
Ady Griffiths, 2020.

Mindful Thoughts for Gardeners:
Sowing Seeds of Awareness
Clea Danaan, 2018.

Mindful Thoughts at Home: Finding
Heart in the Home
Kate Peers, 2020.

Mindful Thoughts for Makers:
Connecting Head, Heart, Hands
Ellie Beck, 2019.

Mindful Thoughts for Mothers: A
Journey of Loving-awareness
Riga Forbes, 2019.

Mindful Thoughts for Runners:
Freedom on the Trail
Tessa Wardley, 2019.

Mindful Thoughts for Sailors: Wind,
Water & Wellbeing
Kitiara Pascoe, 2022.

Mindful Thoughts for Stargazers:
Find your Inner Universe
Mark Westmoquette, 2019.

Mindful Thoughts for Students:
Nurture Your Mind, Flourish in Life
Georgina Hooper, 2021.

Mindful Thoughts for Surfers:
Tuning in to the Tides
Sam Bleakley, 2020.

Mindful Thoughts for Walkers:
Footnotes on the Zen Path
Adam Ford, 2017.

OTHER CONSCIOUS LIVING TITLES

Jessica's Raw Chocolate Recipes
Jessica Fenton, 2011.

Let's Wildflower the World: Save,
Swap and Seedbomb to Rewild
our World
Josie Jeffery, 2022.

Sleep Tight: Illustrated Bedtime
Stories & Meditations to Soothe you
to Sleep
Alison Davies, 2021.

The Writer's Creative Workbook:
Finding Your Voice, Embracing
the Page
Joy Kenward, 2019.

Yoga Asana Cards: 50 Poses &
25 Sequences
Natalie Heath, 2022.

WELLNESS RESOURCES

'We read books to find out who we are.' Ursula K. Le Guin

BOOKS THAT ENLIGHTEN

Feelings: A Story in Seasons
Manjit Thapp, Random House,
2021.

*Finding Peace: Meditation and
Wisdom for Modern Times*
Lama Yeshe Losal Rinpoche,
Penguin, 2021.

*Grounded: A Companion for
Slow Living*
Anna Carlile, QUBM4, 2020.

*Losing Eden: Why Our Minds Need
the Wild*
Lucy Jones, Penguin, 2020.

*The Novel Cure: An A–Z of
Literary Remedies*
Ella Berthoud & Susan Elderkin,
Canongate Books, 2013.

*Plant Magic: Herbalism in Real
Life*
Christine Buckley, Shambhala
Publications, 2020.

*The Spirit Almanac: A Modern
Guide to Ancient Self-care*
Emma Loewe & Lindsay
Kellner, Tarcherperigee, 2018.

*Wintering: The Power of Rest
and Retreat in Difficult Times*
Katherine May, Ebury, 2020.

PODCASTS TO TUNE INTO

Dream Fuel with Arlo Parks
https://www.bbc.co.uk/
programmes/m0016c3d

The Self-Love Fix
https://selflovefix.libsyn.com

FILMS TO BOOST
YOUR MOOD

The Best of Enemies, 2019.

Green Book, 2018.

Untouchable, 2011.

POETRY TO UPLIFT YOU

*The Poetry Pharmacy: Tried-and-
True Prescriptions for the Heart,
Mind and Soul*
William Sieghart, Particular, 2017.

The Sun and Her Flowers
Rupi Kaur, Simon & Schuster, 2017.

*Where Hope Comes From: Poems of
Resilience, Healing and Light*
Nikita Gill, Orion, 2021.

MAGAZINES & JOURNALS
TO NOURISH YOUR MIND

Bloom
Breathe
Ernest
Flow
Mantra Wellness
Origins
Wonderground

INDEX

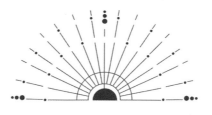

ABOUT RALU

Raluca Spatacean is a Romanian illustrator who is inspired by the balancing elements of wellbeing and the natural world. In 2013 she decided to follow her intuition and creative instincts to travel the world – living in Italy, Spain, Romania, Ireland and England – and experience living life with freedom and joy. In 2020 and throughout the global pandemic, she put pen to paper and discovered the joy of digital illustration which she started to share with the world on Instagram, and soon found a dedicated community of followers soothed by her calming, positive artworks and writings.

@madebyralu

Leaping Hare Press

ABOUT LEAPING HARE

Leaping Hare Press creates beautiful books to inspire and empower readers to translate ethical and spiritual values into practical, meaningful life choices. Exploring MBS, self-help, nature, esoterica and creativity, our books present creative, simple steps to help us engage with each other and the natural world. Penned by heart-led and expert authors, our conscious living titles embrace community spirit and explore ecological principles in a positive way – delivering that feel-good factor too.

Thank you to all of our beautiful Leaping Hare Press authors – past, present and future – who together have created the heart and spirit of the list.